Advanced Tarot

A Simplified Guide
to
Universal Symbols

By

Shé D'Montford

A **Special Thank You** to Katrena Rose who pushed me into compiling this deck and accompanying book. When I delayed, Katrena was not put off by my excuses of being busy or involved in a time consuming T.V. show, she continued to poke me and prod me until you have this version in your hands today. It originated as a PowerPoint presentation that I have used for years to teach professional Tarot readers. After assisting me on one of my workshops, Katrena remarked what a comprehensive book and deck it would make and how easily, in theory, it should convert from one medium to another. Yet, it took over a year of blood, sweat, and tears. Katrena's insights during the process were so valuable and juxtaposition mine so well, we have decided to include them in this work too. I hope that you enjoy this deck and book more than we enjoyed converting it from PowerPoint to printed matter.

Thanks to Robert Bruce Spackman for proof-reading and editing the things in this 2nd edition that an author never sees as she reads what she expects that she has written.

And of cause Many Blessings & Thanks to you "The Reader"

Shé

Advanced Tarot, A Simplified Guide to Universal Symbols by Shé D'Montford ISBN: 978-0-9943541-6-7
Information about Shé D'Montford's authorised "Talking Tarot" & "Advanced Tarot" workshops z
& "The Talking Tarot" Tarot Deck
are available from Shambhallah Awareness Centre,
a tax exempt Pagan Church and a not for profit organisation
P.O. Box 3541, Helensvale Town Centre. Q. 4212
w w w . s h a m b h a l l a h . o r g   &   w w w . s h e d m o n t f o r d . c o m

Advanced Tarot, A Simplified Guide to Universal Symbols by Shé D'Montford ISBN: 978-0-9943541-6-7
Dr. Shé D'Montford's The Talking Tarot - Speaking The Language of Universal Symbols - Written By Rev. Dr. S. D'Montford additions by Katrena Rose - Cover Artwork and Graphic Artwork By Rev. Dr. S. D'Montford © Copyright Rev, Dr S. D'Montford, Friday, August 15, 2008 Gold Coast Australia. Published by Shambhallah Awareness Centre.

Additional Thanks to: -
My long-suffering family, Channel 7, & Wiki-Media Images, last but never least, my loving partner Ken Wills.

Advanced Tarot

A Simplified Guide
to
Universal Symbols

By

Shé D'Montford

CONTENTS

The Major Arcana   **31**

The Minor Acana   **55**

The Suit of Wands   **58**

The Tarot is The Language of The Universe in Symbols

No spiritual education is complete until you learn this language. Yet, you do not have to stumble through this learning curve alone as I did. This deck will tell you how.

The word "Orat" is Latin for "It speaks" and taro (phonetic) spelt backwards. This is a plain speaking deck designed to aid your mystical comprehension. Each of these Tarot cards clearly displays its own common and deeper meaning in words along with its number, planetary, hermetic, monad, and Cabalistic correspondences. Each card also lists archetypal associations from which you may draw on the wealth of mythic law and history to deepen your perception. To aid your subconscious associations, carefully chosen colours and iconic images have been selected to illustrate each major arcana card. Court cards are well known contemporary and historical figures that embody that particular energy as they were in the original Tarot. The suits in this deck stick with the original traditional logos that have so accurately spoken to people for millennia. Though it implies symbolic representation, "logos" is Greek for "word" and where we derive the term "language." To help you grasp this universal symbolic language, this accompanying book also has a whole page dedicated to each card, with interpretations from Katrena and myself, refined from our combined 70+ years of experience reading Tarot. Utilising all these tools enables this Tarot deck to begin talking to you in a language you can understand, immediately.

The Bodet Tarot -Circa 1400

The Origin Of The Tarot Cards

The origin of the tarot cards are shrouded in Mystery. Western history's first documented Tarot deck is 'Visconti-Sforza Tarocchi' cards in Italy in the middle ages. Yet the symbolism expressed in the images are connected to the ancient mysteries of the Egyptian Hermetic initiation rites.

Recent discoveries in China and India of decks of cards containing the same symbology yet dating back thousands of years, indicates that the Gypsies, in their migration from India to the middle east and then to Europe, may have spread the Tarot's usage in their wake. The word "Taru" means "Cards" in both the Hindu, and Gypsy/Rom/Sinto languages.

The Sacred Book Of The Gypsies

Indeed the Tarot is often referred to as "The Sacred Book Of The Gypsies." Legend states that the clever gypsies converted their most sacred book to symbols when their texts were banned. They then converted it further to a set of playing cards, which became fashionable in the royal courts, thus hiding their ancient wisdom in plain sight.

Your Spiritual Journey

Knowledge of the Tarot can help you understand your journey through life. All humans, no matter what culture or tribe they are from can identify with the symbols that illuminate the Tarot. Because of this, Jungian psychology uses these archetypal Tarot images in their methods. The Tarot signposts our individual passage through existence, thus these images occupy our collective subconscious. Like steps taken down a path, one follows the other. We must progress, whilst continuing our soul's spiritual expedition, through these milestones. Everything in the universe has it own pace of progression on this trek, dependant on knowledge acquired. Each individual Tarot card equates to a book of the knowledge to be acquired on this spiritual adventure. A good Tarot reading will allow you to see where you are on this journey. A spread creates a life map that illustrates both where you are right now and what you are likely to encounter a little further down the road.

Tarot Readings

The skilled reader looks at the personal map laid out in the spread of their client and can tell them what points of interest they will encounter next, what is in store for them, where they have been and ultimately, if they stay on this chosen path, where they will arrive.

Are there enough combinations of cards for every person to have an individual reading? Using only the 22 cards of the Major Arcana by themselves there are 727,000,777,607,680,000 possible combinations. That is some 100,000 times the Earth's population, and that is not even dealing with a full deck!

If we use the full 78 cards of the Tarot to calculate this statistic, the page could not contain all of the zeros needed to express that number nor could our mind comprehend it. As we only have 6,000,000,000 people alive on the planet, you can see how there is plenty of room for each individual to find their personal life map illuminated in The Tarot.

Tarot Facts at a Glance:

- The deck is composed of 78 cards.
- These are divided into 22 Major and 56 Minor Arcana cards.
- The Major Arcana are composed of 22 cards numbered 1-21 and one unnumbered card (0) called The Fool, symbolising the human condition as it exists before setting foot on the path.
- The Minor Arcana are divided into 4 suites Cups, Swords, Pentacles, and Wands.
- Each suite has numbered cards from 1 - 10 plus a King, Queen, Knight and Page.
- The Minor Arcana are the origin of contemporary playing cards in use to this day.

The Marseille Tarot

The Marseille Tarot or Tarot of of Marseilles was for centuries the standard pattern for the design of tarot cards. From the 1400s to today.

It is a pattern from which subsequent tarot decks derive. it only has elemental number symbols on the four standard suits. Bâtons (Batons), Épées (Swords), Coupes (Cups), and Deniers (Coins). The four suits represented the for elements that make up the material world. Air Fire Water and Earth respectively.

Suits				
ENGLISH NAMES	Wands	Swords	Cups	Penticles
TRADITIONAL FRENCH NAMES	Batons	´Eoées	Coupes	Deniers
ELEMENT	Air	Fire	Water	Earth
DIRECTIONS	South	North	East	West
TIMING	Days	Weeks	Months	Years
ZODIAC	Aquarius Libra Gemini	Aries Sagittarius Leo	Pisces Cancer Scorpio	Capricorn Taurus Virgo

As well, there are four court cards in each suit: a Valet (Knave or Page), Chevalier or Cavalier (Horse-rider or Knight), Dame (Queen) and Roi (King).The court cards are sometimes called Les Honneurs (The Honours) or Les Lames Mineures de Figures (The Minor Figure Cards) or the "Royal Arcana" in English. The suit of batons is drawn as straight objects that cross to form a lattice in the higher numbers; on odd numbered baton cards, a single vertical baton runs through the middle of the lattice. On the tens of both swords and batons, two fully rendered objects appear imposed on the abstract designs. The straight lined batons and the curved swords represented scimitars and the batons polo mallets. Cups and coins are drawn as distinct objects. Most decks fill up blank areas of the cards with floral decorations. There are also the twenty-two atouts (trump cards). The Fool, which is unnumbered and twenty-one numbered trumps because it usually cannot win a trick. These twenty-two cards were called Les Lames Majeures de Figures (The Major Figure Cards) or Arcanes Majeures (Major Arcana) in French.

The Ryder-Wait Deck

The Rider-Waite tarot deck, originally published 1910, has become the most popular style tarot deck in use for divination in the English-speaking world. The cards were originally published in November, 1909 by the publisher William Rider & Son of London. In the book written to accompany the cards, he failed to mention the artist, Pamela Colman-Smith, by name, saying only that a *"young black woman artist had illustrated them upon his instructions."* This dismissive attitude is inexcusable as they were equal members of the same fraternal Order since 1901. Pamela had been a full member of the Order of the Golden Dawn right along with the better known members such as William

Butler Yeats and Florence Farr. She was a senior founding member of the 'Hermetic Order of the Golden Dawn' before Arthur Waite caused his faction. Coleman-Smith originally met Waite through the Golden Dawn occult organisation. Together, they would create one of the world's most popular tarot decks. Many tarot historians believe that the lion's share of the credit for the deck actually belongs to Coleman-Smith for the artwork and the authorship too. Waite admits that he only carefully controlled the creation of three cards:

"I saw to it that Pamela Coleman [sic] Smith should not be picking up casually any floating images from my own or another mind. She had to be spoon-fed carefully over the Priestess card, over that which is called the Fool and over the Hanged Man."

In contradiction to this, letters survive in which Waite sends Coleman-Smith to the British museum to make sketches from an Italian tarot deck from the 1400's The Solar Busca Tarot, on display there, with permission for the collector and in this letter Waite asks Colman-Smith for her interpretation of the meanings of each of the cards.

In order to gain permission from his Order to publish the he had to promise not to release any true mysteries taught to him by them. To do this he reversed the numerical position on two of the major arcana cards, 8 Justice and 11 Strength. This throws out the numerical symmetry of the deck. There are 3 evenly spaced immortal cards in the deck, Strength being one of the immortal cards. 1 The Magician, the masculine immortal, 11 Strength The feminine immortal, and 21 The World the Androgynous immortal. 8 Justice is not an immortal card.

Additionally he reverse the elemental attributions of Air, Wands and Swords Fire, which can seriously throw out the information that can be gained from the   previous table of correspondences for the minor arcana. In his book to accompany his deck he dismisses these prostitutions of the Tarot by saying: "The average reader is not intelligent enough to understand why the change had to occur." We understand Mr Wait, you did it for money!

Unfortunately most modern tarots decks have literally followed suit. You can still do accurate readings with your best loved decks but you need to know the correct correspondences to do so.

The Numbering System

The word 'Tarot' means 'to turn or rotate.' The Tarot is book that is all about the turning of cycles of time. A way to travel through time if you will and therefore predictive. As a consequence, altering numbering system in a tarot deck is criminal, as it renders the deck's cyclic predictive ability virtually useless.

Time, is of a necessity, measured out into incremental numerical portions. The major arcana shows the soul's journey through a lower and higher time cycle to the point of self-realisation. (The World Card) The union of two sets of the cycle of ten for the material world and three sets of seven for the spiritual world make up the cycle of twenty-one numbered cards in the major arcana.

Plus there is a numberless beginning card - the no name card, the nothing, the potentia, the great ZiGi, the card without a number, the zero.t(The Fool.) Science is now only beginning to discuss this full nothingness from which all things are created. The discovery and study of dark matter and dark energy in 2003 has been shown to exist in the micro and macro space between all matter and time.

Pythagorean Monads

Pythagoras is famous for teaching that numbers are alive and are part of nature. They are alive. They dive, they multiply, they grow, they decline. They are spirits in their own right. Pythagoras taught that these intelligent numbers want to help you solve all of life's problems.

This can be especially true for quitrents of The Tarot.

The first ten digits were especially sacred and thought of as deities in their own right, called "Monads."

The Emerald Tablet says: "From the one the many arise." This is the origin of the Ennead, (the nine plus one) the ten archetypal gods in Egyptian, Greek and Norse heaven.

Pythagoras showed these monad spirits to be numerical in nature and attributed them the following personalities and symbols:

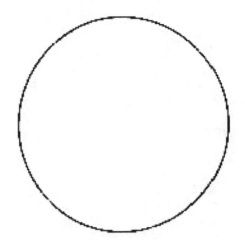

THE MONAD

- Proteus - The First - The Ultimate Prime
- Male-Female
- The Seed - The All
- The Fabricator
- Oneness of mind
- The Demiurge
- Zeus - Life God - Ra
- Memory
- A vehicle
- Blessedness
- Eudaimonia - True Happiness - human flourishing -prosperity
- Ousia -Essence
- Pandokeus - The Inn Keeper - That Which Takes in All
- Paradieigma -The Pattern or Model
- Prometheus - The Moulder - The Shaper
- The Obscure - Darkness
- The immutable truth and the invulnerable destiny

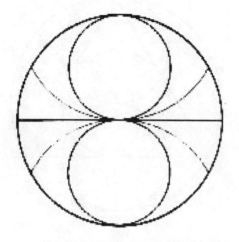

THE DYAD

- Female
- Double
- Equal
- Aorlstos - The Indefinable
- Apeiron - The Unlimited
- Birth & Growth
- Appearance
- Anguish
- Movement
- Logos - The Ratio
- Analogia - Proportion
- Revolution & Obstinacy
- The thing with another
- Isis - Slene - Rhea (the wife of Cronus also know as "The Flow")
- Combination
- Tolma - Boldness - Audacity
- Matter & Nature

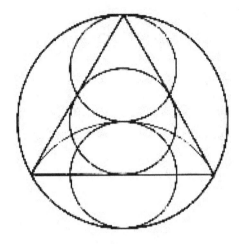

THE TRIAD

- Male
- Triple
- Inequality
- Disproportion Harmoni
- Gnosis - Knowledge
- Peace
- Everything
- Hecaté
- Good Council
- Piety
- The Mean Between the two
- 1st Initiation
- Friendship
- Purpose

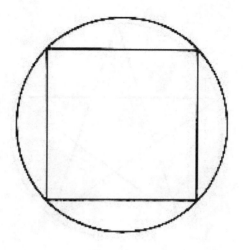

THE TETRAD

- Rightness
- Righteousness
- Right Angles
- Hercules
- Holding the Key of Nature
- Building
- Artificial construction
- The Nature of Change
- Inflexibility
- Insecurity
- Instability
- Impermanence
- Death

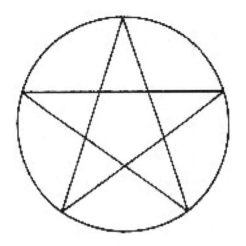

THE PENTAD

- Androgyny
- The union of the first masculine & famine principles
- Wedding - Marriage
- Aphrodité - BouBastia (the Egyptian Deity of pleasure)
- Procreation
- Creation -Procreation - Alteration -Immortality
- The Phi Ration - Fibonacci
- Lack of strife
- Manifesting Justice
- Pallas - Nemesis - Themis
- Demi God
- Five fold thought
- Light
- Material Life

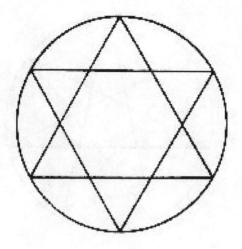

THE HEXAD

- The Brother
- The Helpful One
- Service
- Apollo - Far Shooting - (Apollo's epithet)
- Amphiitrite - Poseidon's wife (A Greek verbal pun on both sides (Amphis) & three (Triasl)
- Finest of all
- In Two Measures
- Forms of forms
- Double Peace
- Thalia
- Possessing Wholeness
- Panacea - Cure all
- Perfection
- Three fold Health
- Reconciling
- Remembering Justice
- The Thunder Stone

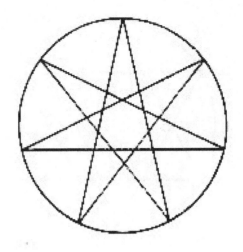

THE HEPTAD

- The Sister
- The Mystical One
- Septa's Sebomai Heptas - The Revered Seven
- Athena - The Forager - (Ahthena's epithet)
- Artist
- Seeing the unseen
- Emotional bias - seeing things as better or worse than they are
- Koré - Persephone - Virgin - Maiden
- Luck
- Fortune
- Fate
- Acropolis - Citadel
- Reaper
- Hard to subdue
- Kairos - Due Measure
- Telephorus - Bringing to completion
- Preserving

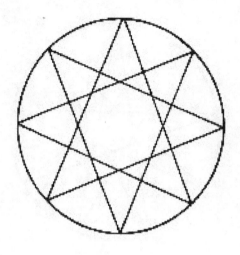

THE OCTAD

- Mother
- 2nd Initiation
- All Harmonious
- Steadfast
- Seat- Abode
- Womb of Creation
- Home
- Earthly
- Prosperity
- Music
- Euterpë, the Muse of lyric poetry
- Spontaneous
- Untimely Born - Lucky birth -
- Cadmia - a term in Alchemy when doing one thing and something else useful but unexpected happens - Literally a calming oxide of zinc, applied to the skin for irritations (calamine lotion) a byproduct of creating things in a smelting furnace
- Hephaestus - The Smith god

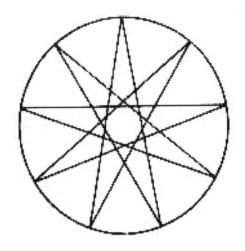

THE ENNEAD

- Consort
- Near Completion
- Eos - The New Dawn
- Hera
- Assimilation
- Reconciliation
- Focus
- Horizon
- Crossing or Passage
- Working at bringing something to perfection
- Recovery
- Telesphorus -"the accomplisher" or "bringer of completion" son of Asclepius- his sister, Hygieia. He symbolised recovery from illness.
- Hyperion -he who brings in a new era
- Oceanus - genesis for all - encircling the earth

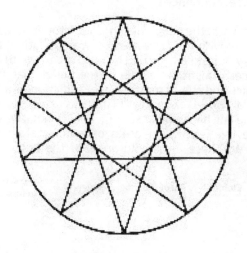

THE DECAD

- The Father - God
- Level Up
- Aeon - A Measure of Eternity
- Uniting all below in One above
- Atlas
- Fates
- Key-Holding
- Kosmos
- Strength
- Memory
- Ourania Ράνια, Rania, Ranya "of heaven" the muse of astronomy
- Heaven
- All
- Perfect
- Phanes - the mystic primeval deity of procreation & the generation of new life
- New Phases

Elemental Correspondences

When working with the elements in The Tarot it is easier and more accurate to work with the 'Five Areas of Manifestation' rather than the seven bodily chakras and their plethora of popularised correspondences. This is reflective of the belief that five, along with all its harmonics and sub-harmonics, are reflective of all manifestation in the material world of matter. This was a deeply held belief by Pythagoras and all hermeticians. N.B. This is not the chakra system. These are the five Tattwas or areas of manifestation of the physical plane of matter. These are whole areas of the body and not just an

Tattwa	Element	Tarot Symbol	Meaning	Area of Manifestation	Associated colour & shapes
Prithivi	Earth	Pentangles	Material things, Money Prosperity Wellbeing	Bottom of Feet to Knees	Yellow & Square
Apas	Water	Cups	Emotional states	Knees to Groin	White Crescent Moon
Tejas	Fire	Swords	Passion, Drive, Determination	Groin to Solar Plexus	Red Fire Triangle
Vayu	Air	Wands	Work or what they do	Solar Plexus to Throat	Blue Air Circle
Akhasa	Spirit	Court Cards	Internal evolution or others around querent	Throat to top of the head	An Egg the colour of Darkness or Octerine

energy centre located at a point inside, that controls some of the internal organs. The areas of manifestations are how we create, mould and move through this worldAkasha/Quintessence/Dark Matter, the substance of which all things in the universe are made, are represent by the four court cards of each element.

Colour Correspondences
As can be seen from the previous chart, colour can have meaning and can stimulate the intuition. Tarot decks have been traditionally printed in the 7 basic primary and secondary colours.

Here follows the means of the basic colour spectrum:

Red: Passion, Drive, Determination, Hunger, Lust, Settling Down, Play

Orange: Creativity, Fertility, Birth, Spirituality, Deity, Strength, Perfect souls

Yellow: Attention, Ego, Self-Centredness, Power, Fun, Performance, Acting

Green: Heart, Health, Love, Growth, Balance, Attraction, Nurturing

Blue: Mind, Intellect, Communication, Concepts, Ideals - Ethics, Freedom, Melancholy

Indigo: Third Eye, Hormones, Unity / Oneness, Manifesting, Veil between the worlds, Angelic Realms, Magick

Violet: Crown, The Realms Above, Deity, Transcendence, Akasha / Knowing, Intuition, Right Action

—————————————————

Ok so lets start to put all of this information together in a way that is meaningful to you and to your clients.

Tarot Spreads

When you decide to do readings, the spread that you use for the cards is just as important as the cards themselves. A spread is like a map to the buried treasure in each individual's life. It reveals the answers they are looking for and directs the reading's energy and outcome. It is important to choose a spread that will answer the questions your being asked. For example. if you or your client wants an overall look at what is going in their life right now, you would use a general spread, like 'The Wheel' or 'The Celtic Cross.' Whereas if you or your client wants a reading focusing on particular question like romance or finances you would use a more specific spread like 'The True Love Spread' or 'The Solutions Spread.'When you lay out your Tarot cards in a spread you are choosing one area to focus on for each card. For example, with 'The True Love Spread' the first card is The Message Card, which is a card that gives you a message from spirit about your love issues. Whereas the second card represents your subconscious desires from love relationships. Therefore, if the Lovers Card fell in the first position you would read it as a message to look deeper as your partner could be involved with someone else. Yet, if the Lovers fell in the second position you would need to look at your own level of commitment or you may be straying from the relationship.

When you choose the design of a spread, it is important to think about what questions you want answered and how you want to lay out the cards. For example if you want a brief look into some issue, then one to three cards would be plenty, but if you want lots of information and to understand the energy or reasoning behind something, then more cards will be necessary. Take time to think of the design of your spread before you use it. Meditate on it and think about the subject matter of the reading, i.e. what you want to find the answers to. A meditation on the spread and how it flows is also important to get it feeling right and answering your questions accurately. The number of cards in each spread is usually suggested by the spirit whilst in meditation, but you can also use numerology to help if you like. Seven being a lucky number and a magical number would be a great amount of cards for a reading on finances or psychic/spiritual development. Whereas, three is a great number for parties and business deals and ten is a good number to gain a complete snapshot picture of the querent's whole life. You will soon notice that each spread has its own flow and thought provoking aspects that will teach you more about reading Tarot.

THE PYTHAGOREAN 10 CARD SPREAD
or
THE TRADITIONAL CELTIC CROSS METHOD

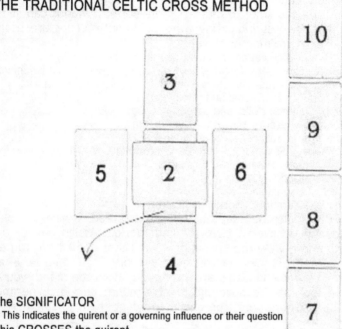

1. The SIGNIFICATOR
   This indicates the quirent or a governing influence or their question
2. This CROSSES the quirent
   This is not going well or working against the will of the quirent
3. This CROWNS the quirent
   This is the best influence at the moment
4. This SUPPORTS the quirent
   A supporting influence from which they can draw strength and stability
5. This is BEHIND the quirent
   The quirent's recent past
6. This is BEFORE the quirent
   The quirent's near future
7. The QUIRENT
   Personality traits of the quirent they have or need or that are blocking them attaining their objective
8. The ENVIRONMENT
   Factors in the environment around the quirent that are affecting the question
9. The EMOTION
   Emotional factors in play affecting this question
10. The FINAL OUTCOME
    The outcome if the quirent changes nothing and stays set upon the path they are on

The Wheel

'The Wheel Spread' is a great general reading spread. Arrange these cards in a circle from 1 -12 like a clock face. This reading is also good for getting answers on questions of timing. E.g. "How long before X happens?" You can use the positions to indicate how may time-increments, and the suits to indicate time-periods. Wands can signify days to weeks, swords indicating weeks to months, cups are usually months and coins are months to years.

1. *You Now* – Your physical environment and attitudes
2. *Possessions* – Short-term finance, buying, selling, and personal belongings.
3. *Communications* – Your communication skills and advice from spirit.
4. *Home & Family* – Your home and family issues.
5. *Creativity* – Talents, skills, and parenting issues.
6. *Health* – diet, exercise, and general wellbeing.
7. *Relationships* – Romance, love, and marriage.
8. *Sex and Money* – Sexual Issues and Long term finances
9. *Travel and Study* – Holidays and Education
10. *Career* – Ambition and Authority issues.
11. *Inner Self* – Personal and Emotional Self.
12. *Spirituality* – Karmic Reflection and Faith.

'The Wheel' can also be adapted as a great spread to have a look at what is coming up over a twelve-month period. Assign one card to each month and review the upcoming year. These don't have to be in numerical order of the months e.g. January = 1 June = 6 and December = 12. You can also start the reading from the month you are in now and look at the upcoming twelve-month period. Experiment with your spreads and don't be afraid to adapt them to suit the way you like to work.

True Love Spread

Lay these cards out in a line from left to right

1. *The Messages Card* - A message from spirit about true love issues. This card will reveal any issues or challenges surrounding the relationship.
2. *The Inner Truth Card* – Reveals the subconscious desires concerning love. This card will reveal the inner fears or desires concerning love.
3. *The True Love Card* – This card gives a description of the true love partner. Revealing if the client has found the right one or describing the future partner.
4. *The Partner Card* – One partner's role within the relationship. This card will explore the things one partner contributes to the relationship.
5. The Client Card - The other partner's role within the relationship. This card will explore the things the other partner contributes to the relationship.
6. *The Relationship Card* – This card reveals any karmic, past-life or soul purposes from the relationship. Giving you the reasons why you chose each other and how the relationship will fare long term.

The Solution Spread

Lay these cards out in a line from left to right
1. *The problem or issue that is being asked about.* This card reveals the current challenges and the question being asked.
2. *Outside influences.* This card indicates the other factors that are involved concerning the issues and other people's influences.
3. *Action needed.* This card gives you the solution to the issues currently and gives you the steps to find a solution.
4. *Outcome.* This card describes the final outcome if the action needed is taken.

Interpreting the Tarot Reading

Interpreting a reading begins with a clear mind and a positive attitude. Whether reading for yourself or another you should take three to ten deep breaths first and be as calm and clear as possible. People should have a reading feeling positive. You can lift their energy and help others become aware of the level of control and talents they have available to them in their lives. A Tarot reading can be a release of past limitations and a glimpse of what an individual can achieve in the future. If you are not focused and in a positive frame of mind then you are only going to recognise more negative energies around yourself or the person you are reading for. The best way to clear your mind before doing a reading is to have drink of pure water and use a moment of meditation and deep breathing. Ask spirit to help you give a clear and positive reading.

Usually we can be very honest with ourselves. However, we are not too happy when someone else tells us about our own failings. Always be tactful and never scare your client. As a Tarot reader, it is important for you to be able to recognise positive and negative energy flows and blocks within yourself and others. If you can understand where the person you are reading for is coming from, then you can better understand their challenges and beliefs, therefore enabling you to give a useful, positive, and enlightening reading.

- Contributed by Katrena Rose

The

Major

Arcana

0 - The Fool
The Spirit of Beginnings

Card Number: 0

Rulership: Chaos

Key Words:
Learn. Don't be foolish. Don't act impulsively
Don't take a false step

Divinatory meaning:
Choices. Naïveté. Overt innocence. Lack of Common sense. Beginnings. Journeys. Personal Development. Growth. New cycle. Energy. Force. Blithe happiness. Pollyanna optimism. Spontaneity. Change. New Job. Overturning the status quo. Important decisions.

Ill Dignified:
Foolishness. Caution. Ill advised. Risks. Impulsiveness. Rash decisions. Gambling, Instability. Waste. Frittering away resources. Bad time for commitments.

Layers:
The holy fool runs cross cultures. Mania, madness, hysteria, and frenzy were all used as sacred tools to reach the realms of the gods. The spiritual path is not considered the sanest choice. Loosing it helps you find it.

Artwork Archytype: Dionysian Manade

With: -
Ace rods or
3 Coins or
3 Wands = Don't Jump into a New Business

Ace Cups or
2 Cups or
Emperor / Empress = Don't jump into a new romance

Ace Swords or
Knight Swords or
Page Swords = Don't be impulsive

Ace Coins - Avoid new risky investments

Temperance or
Judgment or
Chariot or
Wheel of Fortune or
The Tower = Don't resist change. Hold your nose and leap if you have to.

1 - The Magician
The Vortex of Power

I : THE MAGICKIAN
MAGICK DOESN'T JUST HAPPEN; YOU MAKE IT

HERMES. THOTH. MERCURY
YOU HAVE THE TOOLS

Card Number: 1

Rulership: Mercury

Key Words:
Problem Solver - Magic Happens. You can pull a rabbit out of a hat if you have to! 1st key card.

Divinatory meaning:
Education. Apprentice. Initiation. Material world mastery. Creativity. Self-discipline. Your potential. Communication. Wit. Magic. Science. 1st eternal card. You have the tools learn to use them.

Ill dignified:
Your mojo isn't working! Misuse of time or talent. No inspiration. Lazy. Confusion. Hesitation. Poor Communication. Poor co-ordination. Learning difficulties.

Layers:
A key card. Astrology, astronomy, mathematics, cycles, the elements, Heka, hermetics, the Cabala and more. all display the symbols necessary for understanding the Tarot. It is our map showing us where we are in the larger multi-layered universe. Where are we as our cosmic machine spirals through space and time?

Artwork Archytype: Hermies Trismagistus & Thoth

With:
Business Cards - 3 coins 3 wands, 9 cups, = Solving problems in business or for a career

Relationship cards - Ace Cups 10 Cups, 2 Cups, = Solving problems in personal relationships

Family Cards -6 wand, 6 cups, 6 coins = Solving family problems

2 - High Priestess
Priestess of the Silver Star (Intuition)

Card Number: 2

Rulership: Athena

Key Words:
Secrets and Mysteries
Listen to your gut feelings

Divinatory meaning:
Peeking beneath the veil. Intuition. The deeper mysteries. Initiate. Duality. Wisdom. Secret knowledge. Revelation. Hidden influences. The influence of women. Seeking spiritual wisdom.

Ill Dignified:
Cover-ups. Deception. Conspiracies. You cant or won't be shown. Ignorance. Insensitivity. Lack of foresight. Suppression of the feminine. Superficial knowledge. Repression. Feeling uncomfortable with the feminine. Competitiveness. Falling fowl of a strong woman.

Layers:
Wisdom is a woman that keeps her secrets closely guarded. From the ancient curtained tabernacles of the Middle East to the spacious and harmoniously proportioned Parthenon, access to her presences is always restricted yet won by the desire to understand.

Artwork Archetype: Sophia & Athena

With:
Lovers = Use your intuition to make decisions

Chariot = Use your intuition to choose your new direction

Business cards = Use your intuition to make business decisions

Love Cards = Use your intuition with your lovers

3 - The Empress
The Mother of All

3 : EMPRESS
FERTILE ORGANIC CULTURE

APHRODITE ISHTAR; HERA; LUKSHITII
THE STRONG FEMALE

Card Number: 3

Rulership: Venus

Key Words:
Feminine. Natural. Nurture. Fertility. Farm. Fecundity.
The Successful Female – The Good Woman - The Ideal
Woman

Divinatory meaning:
Powerful female figure. Well-being. Comfort. Security.
Creativity. Love. Parenthood. Maternity. Domesticity. Natural. Flowing.
Organic. Cultured. Abundance. Luxury. Growth. Love. Marriage. Pregnancy.

Ill Dignified:
Forced. Unnatural. Relationship/Domestic problems. Lack of affection. Stoic.
Creative blocks. Infertility. Sterility. Promiscuity. Unwanted pregnancy.
Discomfort. Asceticism.

Layers:
Seashells enwrap Aphrodite's sacred form. She rewards the chivalrous that
reverently seek her there. Fatima and Demeter pour their bounty on all with
pleasure. Cupid plays no tricks here. this is natural. Glow with the flow.

Artwork Archetype: Venus/Aphrodite

With :
10 cups = The promotion of well-being and security.
10 coins = domestic stability, abundance and material wealth.
9 cups, = Creativeness in financial affairs, love and parenthood.
World = Maternal care, Fertility, security, achievement of goals and growth.
Sun = marriage and pregnancy.
Strength = Strong successful woman
Emperor = Soul mates

Ill Dignified
5 cups = Possible domestic problems
5 coins = financial difficulties,
3 swords = lack of affection.
2 cups = Creative blocks Infertility

35

4 - The Emperor
The Father of All

Card Number: 4

Rulership: Mars

Key Words:
Masculine. Forced. Will power.
Structure. Synthetic. Engineer. Architect. Builder.
The Good Man – Strong man in business – The ideal man

Divinatory meaning:
Structured. Authority. Government. Corporate. Competitive. Impregnator. Forceful. Development. Planning. Contrived. Artificial. Worldly. Self-control. Experience. Responsibility. Powerful. Ambition. Achievement. Powerful male.

Ill Dignified:
Rebel. Issues with authority figures. Immaturity Indecision. Weakness. Manipulative.

Layers:
Set and Horus struggle yet they confer the Kingship and their praise. Mars protects his children, property, and his citadels. Bastions rise up to guard these things and en-force their right way. Square unnatural constructions stare back at us from his planet. Man will have his way.

Artwork Archytype: Mars/Ares

With : -
5 wands = Competitiveness, ambition
Ace wands = Powerful individuals, forcefulness in development and execution
King swords = Authority, Worldly power, self control
King Wands = structure, governmental and corporate identities.
Strength = Male with the ability to shoulder responsibility
Emperess = Soul mates

Ill Dignified or Reversed -
Justice = Loss or dislike of authority, corporate governmental or parental.
7 cups = Immaturity and indecision.
5 cups = Weakness, manipulative friends or colleagues.

5 - The Oracle
The Voice of Divine Wisdom

Card Number: 5

Rulership: Sun

Key Words:
Divine guidance. The sage advise you need. Know it all.

Divinatory meaning:
The advice you want and need. Wisdom. Ritual. Routine. Religion. Authority. Formal education. Seeker. Lessons. Knowledge. Morals. Ethics. Wise council.

Ill Dignified:
Bad advice. Slander. Propaganda. False first impressions. Distorted truth. Do not sign anything. Misleading advertisements. Unconventionality. Amorality.

Layers:
Ask the questions. ponder the answers. The ancient oracles of the East spread their art Westward. Chinese whispers became great sages. The pillars up hold yet the fissure can plunge. The Popes stole their crown from her. As she held out the olive branch and spoke, her acolytes waited and the priests transcribed and translated to help avoid misinterpretations.

Artwork Archetype: Delphic Oracle

With: -
King wands = Ritual and routine, religious guidance and authority,
Queen wands = education in its formal sense.
High-priestess = A seeker after knowledge and wisdom.
Page wands = Good sound advice, teaching and constructive counsel.
Sun or any of the 5s= Marriage, partnerships and morality.

Ill Dignified -
Page cups = Misleading or dubious advice, poor counsel, slander and propaganda.
9 wands = Beware of first impressions.
5 cups , moon = Distortion of truth and a bad time for signing agreements.
Knight swords = Unconventionality and rejection of family values.

6 - The Lovers
The Children of Choice

Card Number: 6

Rulership: Eros

Key Words:
Choice. Another option. Self-love. Commitment. Family.
When you must decide to go with either the head or the heart, go with the gut!

Divinatory meaning:
Harmony. Union. Choices. Decisions. Test. Use intuition not intellect. Second sight. A struggle between two paths.

Ill Dignified:
Infidelity. Indecisiveness. Contradiction. Deception. Disharmony. Duality. Internal conflict. Romance upsets.

Layers:
Life offers many things. You cannot go will it all. Which to choose? They all seem so alluring. Others will try to influence you by prodding you. Yet, it is your decision. However, choices have consequences. Paris' choice began a 20-year war. Sometimes cupids wings must be clipped and temptation must yield to the self-control of doing what you know is best.

Artwork Archytype: Cupid/Eros

With: -
9 coins = Harmony and union,
High priestess = choices to be made using intuition and not intellect.
9 wands, 7 wands = Difficult decisions to be made not necessarily about love.
5 wands = Some form of test and consideration about commitments.
7 cups = Abstract thought, second sight. Possibly a struggle between two paths.

Ill Dignified -
Moon = Contradiction, deception,
5 swords = disharmony,
2 coins = duality and one's own internal conflict.
2 cups = Infidelity, and romantic disturbances.
Tower = Indecisiveness, postponing choices and a warning not to make important decisions at this time.

7 - The Chariot
Power of Self-Determination

Card Number: 7

Rulership: Sagittarius

Key Words:
Your in the Driver's seat. 1st change card. Gives the individual the most control over their direction - 2012

Divinatory meaning:
Change of direction. Action. Decisiveness. Ambition. Triumph. Victory. Success. Overcoming obstacles. Achieving Goals. Self-control. Effort. Perseverance.

Ill Dignified:
Chaos. Loss of control. Imbalance. Outdated ideas. Cumbersome traditions. Expectations too high. Disregard for others. Envy. Avarice. Destruction.

Layers:
The first leap from the starting post can be chaotic. Steering that burst of energy can be as difficult as herding cats. The irresistibility of Freya and the irrepressibility of Dionysus are unstoppable. Learn the secret of directing this force and your obstacles will be overcome and your treasure will be grasped.

Artwork Archetype: Freya on her chariot drawn by cats

With: -
6 rods = Triumph over adversity, well deserved victory
8 cups = overcoming life's obstacles,
King Coins - decisiveness and ambition in achieving one's goals,.
5 or 7 swords and 7 wands = A period of struggle ending in worldly success.
Queen wands = Self control, effort, perseverance.
10 wands = Working to build up a successful existence.

Ill Dignified-
10 swords = A disregard for others, envy, avarice.
7 swords = Loss of control and chaos in one's personal life possibly due to personal flaws. Devil = Imbalance. Destruction.
5 coins = A warning against overwhelming ambition and high expectations.
Emperor = The continuation of outdated ideas and traditions.

8 - Justice
Lords of Truth and Balance

Card Number: 8

Rulership: Libra

Key Words:
Karma. An even up. Do the right thing.
Life back to balance.

Divinatory meaning:
Triumph. Clarity. Fairness. Arbitration. Conflict resolution. Legalities. Contracts. Settlement. Divorce. Other's judgements of you. Self-judgment.

Ill Dignified:
Injustice. Inequality. Bias. Prejudice. Separations. Delay. Imbalance. Confusion. Tax. Complicated negotiations.

Layers:
The legal system is not the justice system. Toothless tigers have lots of bravado. Yet, what goes around comes around. Justice is blind and insensitive. The weave of the universe must remain balanced. People gather to sit in judgment of another. It makes them feel better than someone else. How heavy is the heart? Will any balance between the pillars against Maat's feather? Our soul cries out for what is only fair. Release the emotional attachment to this and the Karma goes away.

Artwork Archytype: Themis/Maat

With : -
7 swords = Amicable and favourable resolution of conflicts.
6 wands = Triumph over bigotry and prejudice.
Oracle, judgment = Legal action. Litigation. Contracts. Settlement.
Lovers = Divorce. Sometimes marriage depending upon the other cards and normally only when marriage contracts, legal or financial documents are a necessary part of the intended union.
Temperance = Clarity. Fairness. Arbitration.
Sun = A straightforward choice.
Judgment = Judgement.

Ill Dignified-
Devil = Injustice. Inequality and bias.
Lovers = Separations not yet ratified or legalised.
Temperence, 2 swords, 2 coins = Delay. imbalance.
6 coins = tax affairs.

9 - The Hermit
The Sage of the Eternal

Card Number: 9

Rulership: Capricorn

Key Words:
The Solitary Path. Retreat and re-gather your resources.
Time to think.

Divinatory meaning:
Isolation. Retreat. Prudence. Counsel sought. Advice taken. Inner calm. Inner resources. Assimilation. Planning. Spiritual mentor. Stand back and reflect. Share your knowledge whilst seeking more wisdom.

MERLIN; DAKINI; SHIVA
RETREAT & RESTORE TO RADIATE

Ill Dignified:
Ignorance. Advice not taken. Immaturity. Resistance to help. Suspicions. Imprudence. Stubborn self-sabotage. Obstinacy. No one is an island.

Layers:
The inner ear makes us wiser than external learning. Bombarded by noise, radio waves, print, and the world wide web, we could not hear the inner voice if it stood on a mountain and yelled warnings at us. Hearing the calm still voice within requires a healthy period of isolation.

Artwork Archytype: Hermit/Acetic Preist

With:
9 swords = Caution.
3 cups = Discretion.
Temperance = Need for prudence. A wise guide or spiritual mentor.
Oracle = Counsel sought and taken.
Page coins = Planning.
9 coins = Inner calm.
High priestess = A need to reach into one's inner resources.
Moon = Assimilation. A time to stand back and reflect upon circumstances

Ill Dignified -
Page swords = Imprudent actions or decisions, Refusal of counsel or assistance. immaturity.
8 swords, devil = Isolation from others.
10 swords = suspicions about the motives of others.
Ace swords = Foolish obstinacy.

10 - Wheel of Fortune
Rotation of the Forces of Life

Card Number: 10

Rulership: Seasons

Key Words:
Luck favours you. 2nd change card. 2nd Key Card. Less control, but more harmony

Divinatory meaning:
Going with the flow. Effortless success. Good fortune. Coincidences. Luck. New cycle. Advancement. Relief.

Ill Dignified
Swimming up stream. Bad luck. Resistance. Delays. Interruptions. Do not gamble or take risks. Difficulties.

Layers:
Wheels within wheels. Cogs cranking each other through their turns. Seasons and celestial cycles are a part of us. Gearing in with the predominant flow can bring you rapidly to where you want to be. Understand how the wheel turns and you can ride it. Let it lift you rather than grind you. Surf the flows rather than be strapped to the mill. Change your temperature. Is this your spring or fall?

Artwork Archetype: The Wheel of Ixion

With :
9 or 10 cups or 6 wands = Effortless success.
Tower = Good fortune that is unexpected. Positive upheaval. Change.
Any ace = The beginning of a new cycle.
8 coins, king coins = Advancement.
Justice = the appearance of destiny and Karmic change.

Ill Dignified -
Devil, 8 swords, 5 cups = Bad luck that is unexpected.
Ace swords = Resistance to change.
5 cups = Unexpected interruptions.
Temperance = A warning against gambling.
4 cups = Difficulties. Delays.

11 - Strength
The Daughter of Desire

Card Number: 11

Rulership: Leo

Key Words:
Irresistible. Endurance. Be strong, brave and calm.
Don't be afraid to delegate. Accept support.

Divinatory meaning:
Courage. Admiration. Self-control. Fortitude. Love's
power. Energy. Determination. Generosity. Control. Optimism. Resolve.
Fearlessness. Beauty. Radiance.

Ill Dignified:
Misuse of power. Thuggery. Lust. Defeat. Weak-willed. Inadequacy. Pessimism.
Unworthiness. Tyranny. Concession. Lack of action.

Layers:
Gentle water wears away hard stone. Irresistible forces overcome immovable
objects. Femininity before which all men find themselves powerless. The
Goddess at the heart of every woman. Kali and Sekmet are mothers defending
their young, the most terrifying force in nature. Frenzied and instinctual it can
slay all and then gracefully turn to tenderly comfort and feed its crying infant.

Artwork Archetype: Joan of Arc / Durga

With :
Knight wand or swords = Courage.
Hermit = Self control.
2 cups or empress = The power of Sex.
2 swords or 2 coins - Control of passion against one's baser instincts.
Ace swords = Determination.
6 coins = Generosity.
Sun = Energy. Optimism
Judgment = resolve and reconciliation.
Ill Dignified-
Devil = Power wrongly used.
10 swords or page swords = Defeat.
9 swords = Lack of willpower. Feelings of inadequacy.
5 cups = Pessimism

12 - The Hanged Man
The Spirit of Sacrifice

12 : THE HANGED MAN
SUSPENSION; RENEWAL; LEARNING

ODIN; PROMETHEUS; JESUS; MITHRAS
SELF-SACRIFICE MAKES YOU GREATER

Card Number: 12

Rulership: Earth

Key Words:
Hang loose. Wait and learn. Suspension from worries.

Divinatory meaning:
A waiting period. Relief. Inertia. Adaptation. Worthwhile causes. Sacrificing to obtain. Transformation. Inversion. Be patient things are out of your hands

Ill Dignified:
Nothing else can be done right now. Non-committal. Selfishness. Immediate gratification. Apathy.

Layers:
Odin hangs on the world tree around which all life circulates. The orderly world of the cross, the square, and 4 is turned upside down. Sacrificing an eye, he gains the far more valuable magickal vision of the runes. His viewpoint changes. The crows become his new eyes and he sees the weave of the cycles of time clearly. Pausing for thought makes him a great strategist. His suspension and sacrifice has given him wings of new abilities.

Artwork Archetype: Odin on Yggdrasil

With:
6 coins = Devotion to a worthwhile cause.
5 coins = Temporary suspension of progress.
8 cups = Flexibility of mind and a willingness to adapt to changes.
7 coins = Sacrifice in the present to reap benefit in the future.   A waiting period.
Judgment = Rebirth. Transformation.
Tower = Circumstances literally turned on their head.

Ill Dignified or Reversed -
5 coins = Loss.
Lovers = Lack of commitment.
Queen Coins = Preoccupation with selfish and material things.
2 coins = Despite drawbacks a preference for the status quo.
Devil = Oppression.
5 cups = Apathy in pursuit of goals.
Knight swords = Failure to act with an inability to move forward or progress.

13 - Death
Lord of the Gate of Endings

Card Number: 13

Rulership: Pluto/Saturn

Key Words:
Endings. True Change

Divinatory meaning
A new life. Transformation. Change. End of a phase.
Alterations. Transition.

Ill Dignified
Painful or unpleasant change. Face the fear. Inertia. Lethargy. Exhaustion.
Inheritance.

Layers:
All things end. Except for energy and us. Like energy we change state yet are
always here in one form or another. As one incarnation dissolves, another
forms. Without endings, nothing new can begin. Being unaware of the comedy
of the dance of death is a tragedy. How will we handle that change? Will we
choose to leave a little of ourselves behind in this place or will we cut all ties
and move wholly forward. Mahakala and the gods of endings bring their gifts
for our continuance: rest, renewal, experience, rebirth, resurrection, and
money.

Artwork Archetype: Hades/Mahakala

With: -
Any ace or Judgment = The beginning of a new life.
Wheel = Major changes.
8 cups = The end of a phase in life which has served its purpose.
Tower   = Abrupt and complete change of circumstances, way of life and
patterns of behaviour. Alterations.

Ill Dignified -
Ace swords - Death - Be careful
3 swords = Change that is both painful and unpleasant.
7 cups = A refusal to face the fear of change or change itself.
8 swords = Agonising periods of transition.
4 cups = Inertia. Sadness.
5 cups = Lethargy. Mental, physical or emotional exhaustion. Depression.

14 - Temperance
The Lords of Reconciliation

14 : TEMPERANCE
BALANCE; PROPORTION; ALCHEMY

Isis; Ceredwin; Vulcan; Tyr
SELF-CONTROL MAKES YOU STRONGER

Card Number: 14

Rulership: Cancer

Key Words:
Peaceful Balance. Proportionate Distribution.
The reallocation of resources in your life. Making you stronger and more flexible.

Divinatory meaning:
Balance. Combination. Co-operation. Co-ordination.
Diplomacy. Negotiations. Maturity. Even temperament. Good outlook.
Adaptation. Luxury.

Ill Dignified:
Imbalance. Volatility. Poor judgment. Substance abuse. Fickle. Conflicts.
Disagreements. Instability. Combining the wrong elements.

Layers:
The chemistry is right. Isis overseas her craft. Fire with water. Earth and sea.
Male with female. People with each other. The ingredients are brewed and stirred in Ceredwin's caldron. Circe's rough justice and the ethics of Tyr. When the mix is just right it will be magickal. The Valknut draws together and fine-tunes powers from nine worlds. The treads are drawn together and spun without unravelling. Enough is just right.

Artwork Archetype: Hephaestus/Crice

With:
Any of the 2s = Combination. Co-operation. Co-ordination. Innovation through combination.
Queen swords = Diplomacy.
7 swords = Successful Negotiations.
Any of the Kings = Maturity in dealing with certain matters.
Kinght cups = A placid, balanced temperament and good outlook.
9 cups or coins = harmony and balance. good management.

Ill Dignified-
8 swords = An ability to adapt to changing circumstances.
Devil = The continuation of bad habits or unproductive lifestyles.
Page swords, knight swords = Volatility. Poor judgment. fickle decisions.
5 swords = Disagreements.
Knight swords = Restlessness and instability.
Knight coins = trying to combine too many or the wrong elements in too short an expanse of time.

15 - The Devil
The Gates of Matter

IS : THE DEVIL
SLAVISH OBLIGATION; ADDICTION; TRICKERY

LOKIE, ERIS, APEP, CHRONOS
FREE YOURSELF FROM YOUR CHAINS

Card Number: 15

Rulership: Saturn

Key Words:
Chained. Restricted. Trapped. Slavish obligation.

Divinatory meaning:
Mortgages. Debit. Over materialistic. Unhealthy desires. Frustration. Oppression. Hoarding. Sexual obsession. Addictions. Security verses spiritual development. Set healthy boundaries.

Ill Dignified:
Deception. Trickery. Game playing. Abuse of authority. Uncontrolled ambition. Greed. Feeling trapped. Emotional blackmail. Addictive behaviour. A bad person about you.

Layers:
Lokie's tricks can trap. The chaos of Eris can destroy. The great snake Apep seeks to swallow the sun of hope yet the strength of Set prevents him. Be strong. Don't let your hopes die. Only you can allow yourself to be chained into a bad situation.

Artwork Archetype: Loki/Apep

With:
5 coins - Money matters. Feeling the burden of the material side of life.
Queen Coins = Desire for physical and material things.
8 swords = Feeling of frustration and oppression.
4 coins = A tendency to collect and hoard money and material objects.
Strength = Lust. Sexual obsession.

Ill Dignified -
10 swords = True evil.
Any of the kings = Abuse of authority.
10 coins = Greed. Material success is the focus to the exclusion of all other things.
Queen swords = Uncontrolled ambition.
8 swords = Bondage to a person or situation or thing.
2 cups, king cups, queen cups = Emotional blackmail.

16 - The Tower
The Hosts of the Mighty

Card Number: 16

Rulership: Jupiter

Key Words:
Upheaval. Sudden change with no control. Stress. 3rd change card.

THOR; VAJRA DAKINIS; ZEUS
DO YOU WIELD THE POWER ?

Divinatory meaning:
Unexpected change, better or worse. Decisions made for you. Altered lifestyle/residence/job. Upset routines. Consequences. Enlightenment. Clearing debits. Change of mind. Old perceptions fall away. Don't procrastinate. Choose now, you may not get what you want. Which way will you go?

Ill Dignified:
Accident. Imprisonment. Violence. Loss. Ruin. Negativity. Bankruptcy. Disturbance. Disruption. Conflict.

Layers: Where lightening strikes is magickal. Unlimited power is available there. Earth and sky heave and reform. Instant totality. Thor's hammer, created from lightning by the dwarves of inner earth, is invincible. Vajra's caged lightning is freed and she dances for joy. Life is raw, powerful, new and beyond your control.

Artwork Archetype: Thor's Hammer

With:
5 swords = Disruption. Conflict.
Wheel = Major Change. Sudden violent loss.
8 rods or 6 swords = Change of residence, school or job sometimes all at once
Any of the 10s = Overthrow of an existing way of life. Disruption of well worn routines.
5 coins = Ruin and disturbance. Dramatic upheaval.

Ill Dignified -
10 swords = Negativity.
Justice = Restriction of desires and imprisonment.
7 cups = Drastic change that may rob the individual of freedom of expression.
5 coins = Sometimes bankruptcy and imprisonment.

17 - The Star
The Promise of Life

Card Number: 17

Rulership: Inferior conjunction of Venus and Earth, their Phi-ratio dance forms a celestial floral pentagram every eight years.

Key Words:
Your wishes granted. Hope. Harmony. Joy. 2nd chance
1st Blessing card

Divinatory meaning:
Hope. Renewal. Healing. Joy. Happiness. Contentment. Ambience. Glow. Spirituality. Expansion. Promise. Fulfilment. Inspiration. Vigour. Confidence. Protection.

Ill Dignified:
Hopelessness. Self-doubt. Stubbornness. Unwillingness. Inability. Mistrust. Obstacles. Diminished. Rigidity.

Layers:
The morning star appears and the darkest hour is gone. The first rosy tones flush life with glowing beauty. Early bird calls lift pain and sorrow. Mist from the lake makes love to the air in a brief, silent, joyous, sigh. Scarab rolls all the excrement of the world away to the west. Breathe deep. Know that you are alive. Be aglow with spirit.

Artwork Archetype: Flora/Eos/Scarab

With:
9 coins - Healing of old wounds.
2 cups = Spiritual love.
4 or 5 of cups = A mental and physical broadening of horizons.
7 cups = inspiration.
7 swords = Influence over others.
Knight swords = Vigour and confidence.
9 wands = Protection.
Sun, world, 10 cups 9 cups 9 coins = happiness and blessings

Dignifies all other cards

18 - The Moon
Lady of What Lies Beneath

Card Number: 18

Rulership: Moon

Key Words:
Reflection. Contemplation. Seeing/Feeling Deeply.
Deep Waters
Understanding the emotional motivations.

Divinatory meaning
What lies beneath? Intuition. Imagination. The unconscious mind. Dreams. The psyche. Psychic ability. Illusions. Things concealed or hidden from view. Effort required to see things clearly. Pay attention to what needs to be done Fiction writing. Acting. Spying. Secrecy.

Ill Dignified
Deception. Daydreams. Delusion. Lies. Insincerity. Trickery. Depression. Despair. Desperate need for help.

Layers:
Evening comforts, cools and brushes the harshness of the light away. It protects and wraps itself around like a lover. Surrender, disappear, receding into it. What will you find there? Things creep in the pool of reflection. Domesticity howls to the wild side. Unconscious governs consciousness. Which towering twin will you choose?

Artwork Archetype: Diana and Endymion

With : -
7 cups = Imagination. Sometimes signifies fiction writing or acting, particularly work in the entertainment industry.
4 swords = Dreams and psychic impressions.
High priestess = Sometimes psychic work. The unconscious mind.

Ill Dignified -
10 swords = seeing through those who do not wish you well -
Hermit = The need for secrecy.
Lovers = Deception.
3 cups = Insincere people or drunkenness.
5 cups = Despair and a desperate need for help.
Sun = Inability to see things clearly.

19 - The Sun
The Lord of the Fire

19 : THE SUN
OPENNESS & OBVIOUS BLESSINGS

SOL
IT'S ALL IN THE HERE AND NOW

Card Number: 19

Rulership: Sun

Key Words:
Success, Joy and fun.
2nd Blessing Card. Openness.

Divinatory meaning:
Fun. Happiness. Success. Good health. Vitality. Divination. Prediction. Inventions. Academic or scientific achievement. Reward. Acclaim. Approval. Energy. Joy. Marriage. Children. Good muddy, sunny, fun. Blessings.

Ill Dignified
Broken engagements. Relationship difficulties. Autism. Learning disabilities. Allergies. Hyperactivity. Failure. Arrogance. Vanity. Hypersensitivity. Misjudgement. Delays. The sun may bake the mud too dry. Inflexibility.

Layers:
The sun shines on the open hearted. They are its children safe within a protective circle. The universe turns its success towards them the way a sunflower turns to face the sun. Ra watches over and blesses them. Apollo bathes them in music and grants true divination.

Artwork Archetype: Odin & Frig/Isis & Osiris /The Ashvins / The Dioskouroi

With:
10 cups = Contentment and happiness on attaining success.
9 cups = Good Health.
10 coins = Material happiness. Mental, physical and spiritual vitality.
Page wands = New inventors or inventions. Academic and particularly scientific success.
Any of the Kings = Reward. Acclaim. Approval.
Empress or World = Children.
Star = Joy and happiness.
Blessed relationships - 2 cups emperor or empress

Ill Dignified -
Lovers = Troubled partnerships and marriages. Broken engagements and contracts.
7 cups = Sometimes, autism, learning disabilities or allergies. Hyperactivity.
7 cups =   Delayed Happiness.

20 - Judgement
The Spirit of Rebirth and Reinvention

Card Number: 20

Rulership: Saturn

Key Words:
New Beginnings. Rebirth. 2nd chance. Fresh starts.

Divinatory meaning:
Renewal. Changes. Improvements. Satisfactory outcome. Accomplishment. Awakening. Rebirth. Good career moves. Don't judge yourself too harshly.

Ill Dignified:
Stagnation. Delay. Fear of change. Lack of progress. Loss. Separation. Guilt. Don't judge others harshly.

Layers:
Actions have consequences. Right action is rewarding even if it does not bring public accolades. Recognition from your peers and superiors eventually arrives. A new beginning on many fronts. New life, home, career or love. Betterment and a second chance. The dark knight shines in the new day. Osiris rises restored and renewed to weigh the hearts of humans. Release your attachment to emotional conflict and karma flees. Make your choice using your best judgment and act accordingly.

Artwork Archetype: Elenor of Aquitaine/Ostara Hebe/Persephone/Ceridwen

With:
Wheel = Changes and improvements.
Sun = Satisfactory outcome to a specific matter or period of life.   Joy in accomplishment. Awakening. Rebirth.
3 coins, 3 wands, 8 coins = A good time for career moves. renewed,
9 cups = health, vitality and mental clarity.
Lovers = Sometimes indicates important pending decisions that will change the pattern of life for the better.

Ill Dignified -
4 cups, 5 coins =   Delay in concluding a series of actions.
8 swords = Fear of change and sometimes fear of death.
8 cups = Loss and separation, not necessarily permanent.
Justice = Guilt.

21 - The World
The Great Wheel of Time

Card Number: 21

Rulership: Many cycles linked in the Monad Heriogliphica

Key Words:
Success. Completion. 3rd Blessing Card.
Last key card. Last immortal card.
You have all of the elements to get everything that
you want. You just need to put in the effort

Divinatory meaning:
Everything you want will be granted to you. You can have anything you really
want in this world. Accomplishment. Fulfilment. Pregnant with promise. Full
cycle. Success. Culmination.

Ill Dignified:
Frustration. Events have not yet concluded. Hesitation.

Layers:
The threads have drawn together. The elements are in balance. The planets
align. It is all there for our asking. The universe is finite, held together within
the coils of the all-embracing snake. Time cycles, consumes itself, and begins
again. Reality is revealed in its rainbow dreaming. Great mother births
paradise to envelope our world.

Artwork Archetype: Gaia / Hermaphroditus

With:
Dignifies all cards except one = Accomplishment. Fulfilment. Completion of a
personal cycle, project, series of events or chapter in life. Success. A
culmination of events. A sense of repleteness.

Ill Dignified-
Devil = Refusal to taking full advantage of the opportunity. Frustration.
Completion delayed. Sometimes fear of change. Inability to bring something
to a satisfactory end. resistance to change. Lack of trust. An indication that
events have not yet come to a conclusion but are nearing completion.
Hesitation.

The

Minor

Arcana

The Suit

of

Wands

The Suit of Wands

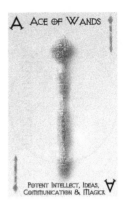

ACE OF WANDS

The Ace of Wands
The Element of Air

Numerical Value: 1

Season: Autumn

Direction: South

Energy: New Ideas

POTENT INTELLECT, IDEAS,
COMMUNICATION & MAGICK

Key Words:
News arriving. Inspiration. Opportunities driving you forward.
New work Opportunities or new things occupying your attention.

Divinatory meaning:
Original ideas. Creativity, inventiveness, Upsurge in intellect. New concept.
Work. A boy. Artistic innovation. New project or career. The essence of air.
Change of mind. Pursuit of truth. Rebirth and a new beginning. Male

Ill Dignified:
Over confidence. Confusion. Exaggeration.

Layers:
Wands direct magickal energy. This requires learning, understanding and lots
of hard work. Electricity crackles. Intellect fires. Connections and correlation
become apparent. The gods of magick bless with intelligence and
communication. They are the spirit of the air. The singular monad signals an
upsurge in this.

With:
Other cards will reveal what you are being or need to be focused on.
With any of the fertility or birth cards can indicate a male baby
Business cards = New business
Health cards = Health improving
7 cups = New creative concepts
Ace swords = Determination to start new things
Ace coins = New venture brings new money

The Two of Wands

Numerical Value: 2

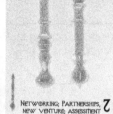

Energy: Waiting

Key Words:
Choices. Alliances.
Management. Working with others. Maximising
potentials

Divinatory meaning:
No one is an island. Beginning success means finding
the right people/organisations to work with. Decisions
need to be made. Success achieved through hard

NETWORKING; PARTNERSHIPS, 2
NEW VENTURE; ASSESSMENT

work. Ideas coming to fruition. Wisdom gained through experience. Wealth obtained legally. Job-related perks.

Ill Dignified:
Ambition. Worthless goal. Sorrow. Illegality. Dishonestly. Deception. Lack of support, teamwork or partnerships.

Layers:
Choosing between and bringing together the right elements. Combining the correct things in the correct proportions is essential to magick, alchemy, and the bubbling cauldron. Finding which works best. Waiting. Watching observing. Drawing together the things needed. Networking the people who will work best with you. The dyad symbolises the energy of combination.

With:
Business cards = it is more who you know that what you know.
7 or 5 swords = Groups plans
2 cups = working with people you love
3 cups = make the right networking connections

The Three of Wands

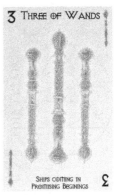

Numerical Value: 3

Energy: Successful ventures

Key Words:
Your ship's coming in. Be ready. Negotiate the next step.
The way is opening

Divinatory meaning:
Dreams turn into reality. Being in the right place at the right time. Successful enterprise. Plans. Ventures. Moving ahead.

Ill Dignified:
Failure to put plans into action. Unattainable goals. A promising enterprise fails. Plans that do not come to fruition.

Layers:
Trinity of power. United forces are legendary. The three sisters and the three musketeers. The polarities and the pivot. Unity in teamwork and balance. Sometimes the injection of a fresh idea can be the life spark of a project. Teamwork and negotiating alliances can generate success. Threes are the first initiatory number. It begins in earnest. The triad symbolises an upsurge in this energy.

With:
Business Cards - Be ready for your opportunity
3 coins = unbeatable opportunities
8 coins = Promotion. Pay rise.
Nine coins = health turning in your favour
Wheel of fortune = Take the risk, it will pay off.

Four of Wands

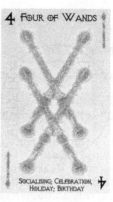

SOCIALISING; CELEBRATION, HOLIDAY; BIRTHDAY

Numerical Value: 4

Energy: Festival

Key Words:
Celebrations. Rewards. Holiday. Things going well for you.

Divinatory meaning:
Celebration. Socialisation. Recreation. Birthday. Wake. Holiday. Holy day. Drinks with friends. Completion of a project. Respite. Endings. Innovator. Designer. The establishment. Splendour. Possible romance.

Ill Dignified:
Partying too hard. Superfluous. Artificial. Constraints. Dogmatic tradition and routine. Reliance upon ceremony.

Layers:
An end has come. Celebrate it. Let go with joyous mourning. The anniversary returns. The setting is constructed. The ceremony begins. The pageantry is beautiful. The bigger the celebration, the larger the after effects. The tetrad represents synthetic construction and man-made artifice, as four is a number that does not often occur in nature.

With:
4 swords = Take a break have a rest
3 cups = go out and enjoy yourself
                    6 cups = family party celebration

Five of Wands

Numerical Value: 5

Energy: Wanting to prove self worth

Key Words:
Self-testing. Passionate responses. Challenges.

Divinatory meaning:
Trying something new. Testing your-self. Possible discord or disagreement. Minor irritations, opposition, trouble strife. Martial arts. Success can be achieved but only through relentless hard work. Excitement. Passionate expressions set you free.

SELF-TESTING; CHALLENGE, STRIFE; QUARREL; GOSSIP

Ill Dignified:
Boredom Micro-management. Domineering. Bullying. Overbearing. Defeat. Hurt. Ruin. Litigation that could be avoided. Spiteful conversation. Unnecessary competitiveness.

Layers:
Loving a challenge we push. Yet there must be resistance to push against. By pushing we test things. Whether in friendly play or life struggle we learn more about ourselves. We realise that we can do more than we ever thought possible. We grow. We begin to trust ourselves. The pentad is growth and marriage.

With :
Page of wands = wanting to learn something new
Queens of wands = wanting to take on tertiary education
5 or 7 swords = planning
7 cups = creative project for recognition
Knight swords = accepting a challenge impulsively
Queen swords = being manipulated into a challenge
6 coins = working for others who are challenged
6 cups = challenged by your past or family

Six of Wands

Numerical Value: 6

Energy: Winning

Key Words:
Victory. Success.

Divinatory meaning:
Triumph. Goals attained. Achievement. The Winners.
Success. Good news.   Public acclaim. Credit.
Recognition. Satisfaction. Obstacles overcome.

Ill Dignified:
Delay. Indecision. Opposition gains the advantage.   Fear of a possible outcome.

Layers:
At last, what you have wanted and what you have aimed for has arrived. By the powers of the air and mind, with the strength of your determination, what you deserve has been recognised. Now you know what it means to hold your head high and move forward in the world. Congratulations. The hexad is the harmonious blending of the elements.

With:
Victory or a win with the energy displayed by any other card

Seven of Wands

Numerical Value: 7

Energy: Overcoming problems or situations

Key Words:
Seemingly insurmountable obstacles easily overcome.
Nothing that you can't handle.

Divinatory meaning:
Gaining the advantage. Successful advancement.
Opportunity requiring skill. Courage and
determination.   Courage in the face of hardship.
Sustained effort brings success. Competition brings out the best in you.

Ill Dignified:
Retreat. Indecisiveness. Challenge lost.   Missed opportunities. Hesitation.
Giving in.   Fear of success. Disputes and disagreements. Deceit used to
manipulate.

Layers:
You are winning the competition but not without struggle or opposition. You
are a step ahead of those who wish you ill. They have tried their best
schemes, you saw through it, predicted their moves and headed them off.
Smile. They will not over come you. However, don't slacken off. The heptad is
the sacred sister of magick.

With:
Any problem card = Don't panic, you can over come this situation.
Any positive card = You will easily achieve this.

Eight of Wands

Numerical Value: 8

Energy: Shifting Energy

Key Words:
Rapid or distant travel – freeing up energy where it
has been stuck

Divinatory meaning:
Sudden or distant travel possibly of your choosing.
Correspondence. Favourable news. Hitting the target.
Rapidly moving towards the goal. Speeding-up. An end
to delays. Take the initiative. Take charge. There is light at the end of the
tunnel.

Ill Dignified:
Running out of steam.   Silly, spontaneous actions.   Cancelled journeys.
Redundancy or sacking. Jumping in before testing the water.

Layers:
The ramifications are far-reaching and rapid. You are moving so quickly you
may not be sure where you will land. The bow was pulled back. You waited
taking careful aim whilst the arrows are sighted. You ached with effort, then
release and the momentum takes your breath away. The octad is abundance
and freedom.

With:
Queen coins = Moving house or renovating
4 swords or wands = Travelling for a holiday
Devil or 8 swords = freeing up areas where you have felt stuck

Nine of Wands

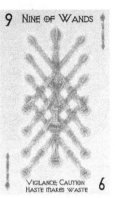

Numerical Value: 9

Energy: Vigilance, Contemplation and watchfulness

Key Words:
Remain Vigilant

Divinatory meaning
Observation. Stability. You are in a good position but stay on the look out. Order. Discipline. Courage. Someone to watch-over you. You are being watched.

Ill Dignified
Destabilised. Impractical. Treachery. Disarray. Insecurity.   Personality flaws. Check your health. Well done, recognition is yours

Layers
When close to a goal caution is often relaxed, that is when set backs can occur. Remain vigilant. You can rest as others look out for you as you have watched over them. However, establish your boundaries. Those who closely scrutinise often become the object of intense observation themselves. The Ennead collects all things together as energy at your disposal.

With:
Any cautionary card = Be careful.
8 Wands or 6 swords = check your travel plans
Any blessing cards = things will work out but don't let you guard down yet or get too flippant.
Any relationship cards = Maintain your guard and make them work hard.
Page cups, 10 swords, Page swords = some one is trying to take advantage of you

Ten of Wands

Numerical Value: 10

Energy: No more

Key Words:
Enough. The reward for hard work well done is...
More hard work!

Divinatory meaning:
Hard work. Methodical. Completion but not an ending. Demands on time. Own business. Work becomes the foremost thing in life. Honourable conduct. Nothing more.

Ill Dignified:
Need to Rest. Laziness. Loss of work. Failure. Jealousy. Micro-management. Inability to delegate. Unnecessary stress. Expansion can exceed the capability to fulfil the demand. Good fortune becomes a burden.

Layers:
To have work is a blessing, laborious but rewarding. After succeeding, people want to give you more work. Over achievers can flourish or buckle at the knees. Listen to your body and your loved ones. What will really give you the greatest happiness right now? More work or rest? The decad completes the cycle.

With:
Other cards indicate a caution to not push yourself too hard in that area.
Ace wands = lots of work or new work – Getting that job or contract

Page of Wands
Feminine Energy under 40
Air
The Concept Guy

P PAGE OF WANDS

SIR RICHARD BRANSON
NEW IDEALIST
d

Energy: Education

Element: Earth of Air

Key Words:
Learning curve. Ideas and enthusiasm. Study. Good news on its way.

Personality Type: Sir Richard Branson

Divinatory meaning
First concept. Starting point. Playful. Inventive. Cheeky. Peter Pan. Messenger of good news. Witty gossip. Diplomatic. Gets to the true nature of things. Negotiator. A good employee. Faithful in service to ideals or superiors.

Ill Dignified
Petulance. Untrustworthy. Delays. Change of address.

Layers
You tell everyone when you find out something marvellous. You pursue your ideals tirelessly. The world is new and wonderful. You flow around useless issues to the simple solutions. You see things as they could be, asking, "Why not?" Pages are new beginnings.

With :
Queen Wands = Tertiary education
4 wands = Teacher
3 wands = New studies
7 wands = Challenging learning curve
4 or 5 cups = not learning - its all too much
Devil or 8 swords = Can't see how it can be done? Change something.
Other cards will indicate what aspect you will be studying.

Knight of Wands
Male Energy under 40
Air
The Intellectual

LEONARDO DA VINCI
CHAMPION OF RENAISSANCE

Energy: Obsessive Determination

Element: Fire of Air

Key Words:
A dog with its bone. The thinker. Achiever of the quest. It can be done!

Personality Type: Leonardo DaVinci

Divinatory meaning:
Clever. Intellect with idealism. Skilful. Active. Perpetual motion. Hard working. Engaging. Think of something and do it. Swift actions that make sense with hindsight.

Ill Dignified:
Irritating enthusiasm. Seemed like a good idea at the time! Arguing just for the sake of it. Strife. Trouble. Discord. Delayed journeys.

Layers:
Anything that you can conceive you can do. Loyalty and justice are major motivators, opportunities and plaudits are secondary. Faithful to the things taught, appreciative of ancient wisdom, yet willing to adapt and innovate. Secrets and confidences are never revealed. Quick to aid a friend or an underdog. Knights are champions.

With:
Other cards show what you are determined about.
8 swords = Stubbornness
Ace swords = single pointed focus on achieving goals

Queen of Wands
Female Energy over 40
Air
The Scholar

QUEEN OF WANDS

HYPATIA
LOVE OF INTELLECT

Energy: Love of Intellect

Element: Water of Air

Key Words:
Attention to detail, Professors, Appreciated for what you do as you do such a good job.

Personality Type: Hypatia

Divinatory meaning:
Success of a project. Independence. Studious. Fair. Intellectual. Beautiful and fertile mind. Conversationalist. Witty. Curious. Social ease. Charm. Idealist. Teacher. Celebrant. Diplomacy. Foresight. Capable. Suffered deep sorrow or loss. Self-awareness. Nurture your ideas.

Ill Dignified:
Pedantic. Scattered. Messy. Domineering. Infallibility. Bitter. Envious. Bigoted. Manoeuvring. Cruel. Sarcasm. Manipulation. Paranoia. One who takes advantage of other's good nature thinking kindness is stupidity.

Layers:
Teachers aren't lovers. Idealists aren't survivors. Pushing for things to be better can sometime make it worse for you. Martyrs irritate, that is why people want to kill them. Queens are the softest form of this energy.

With:
Other cards will indicate what this person is good at.
Page swords or 10 swords = internal politics
Devil or 8 swords = feeling stuck by institutions
6 swords 8 wands = time to move on or do things a new way

King of Wands
Male over 40
Air
The Scientist

Energy: Dominant Intellect

Element: Air of Air

Key Words:
Structured concepts and environments. Large structured organisations.

Personality Type: Pythagoras

Divinatory meaning
Intellectual achievements. Alert. Orator. Writer. High morals with rational. Charming. Responsible. Witty. Comedian. Entertaining. Honest. Conscientious. Judge. Generous. Lawmaker. Inventor. Accountant. Solicitor. Announcer. Philosopher. Miracle worker. Magician. Can debate both sides of an argument and still win. In control.

Ill Dignified
Inability to understand another's point of view. Intolerant of lesser mortals. Narrow minded. Bigoted. Prejudiced. Ruthless. Cares little for the feelings of others. Intolerant.

Layers:
Seeing your way clearly, like a trackless bird in the sky overcomes obstacles and opposition easily. Yet being called upon for an opinion doesn't make you right all the time. Kings are the harshest form of this energy.

With:
Other cards will indicate where structure and order are required or enjoyed

The Suit

of

Cups

The Suit of Cups

The Ace of Cups
Element of Water

Season: Summer

Direction: East

Energy: Loving. Spiritual

Key Words:
A full emotional cup. Love. Fertility. New feelings/
beliefs.

Divinatory meaning:
Romance. Idealism. Optimism. Faithfulness. Fertility. Creativity. Joy. Love. A Girl. An altruistic, creative or artistic project. Intuition. Conception. Fertility. Deep subconscious. Mystery. Feelings. Emotion. Female.

Ill Dignified:
Barrenness, which can be either of a physical or mental nature. Failure of love, stagnation, despair and possibly loss of faith. Illusions. Daydreams.

Layers:
The cup runneth over with all good things. This aces begin the energy of new love. The grail grants the potential to fulfil of all of your desires. The act of selfless tenderness, remembering our heart's need to give and receive, heals the wounded Fisher King. Forgiving ourselves our life is refreshed.

With:
Other cards will reveal what brings you enjoyment.
With any of the fertility or birth cards can indicate a female baby
Business cards = Happy with business
Health cards = Health improving
7 cups = New creative concepts
Ace swords = Determination to start new things
Ace coins = New venture brings new money
Empress = Fertility. Conception. Birth of a child or new creative endeavour.
2 cups = Romantic love

Two of Cups

Numerical Value: 2

Energy: Personal Commitment

Key Words:
True Love. Romance.

Divinatory meaning:
Affection. Love. New romance. Advantageous partnership or friendship. Affinity. Sympathy. Joyous harmony. The reconciliation of opposites in mutual trust. Resolved differences.

Ill Dignified:
Separation. Dissent. Divorce. Deceit. Unfaithfulness. Trouble in a personal relationship. Misunderstandings and quarrels. Love not returned.

Layers:
Contracts are signed. At last both drink the cup of agreement and you are satisfied. Concord at work, within the family or on a personal level. This card is love and romance. Two's are union and partnerships here shared in the deep well of the loving cup. Yet hearts and minds also meet over ideals, passions, interest, inspirations and things that you love and that drive you.

With:
Ace cups = Very romantic time
Lovers = Affair
Any 2s = getting on very well with others
Family cards = Loving family
8 Wands = Romantic travel
4 Swords = holiday
4 wands = Romantic celebration
Sun = wedding or engagement

Three of Cups

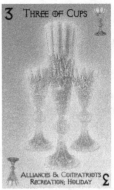

Numerical Value: 3

Energy: Comfort

Key Words:
Networking. Celebration.

Divinatory meaning:
Birthday. Party. Celebration. Commemorating the end of a project or venture. A birth. A new project. Great happiness. A marriage. Abundant fertility. Trust. Harmony. Maternity. Healing. Others that you are comfortable with.

Ill Dignified:
Over-indulgence. Hangover. Selfishness Hedonism. Unhappiness. Famine. Illness. Promiscuity. Obesity.

Layers:
Celebrate good times, come on! We could dance and wildly leap and drain the goblet deep. Or dignified we could network and be quietly self-content within our close circle of friends. When sisters meet in perfect love and perfect trust in the sacred space of a circle all things are possible. Anything can happen and usually does! When males bond it means mates for life. Three is the first masculine number and the first initiation.

With:
2 wands = others creating opportunities for you with work.
4 wands = celebrations of drinks after work
2 cups = friends introducing you to a romantic interest.
2 swords = good strong friendships that you enjoy socialising with

Four of Cups

Numerical Value: 4

Energy: Personal Responsibility

Key Words:
Square peg in a round hole.

Divinatory meaning:
Go with the flow. Don't force things. Don't stay there and get your corners knocked off. Where is the hand of god pointing you? Re-evaluate. Familiarity. Dissatisfaction Boredom. Apathy. Do something more stimulating. Dwelling on past. Reality sets in.

Ill Dignified:
Loss of pleasure. Spoilt. Too much on offer. Listless. Ill health. Fatigue. Overturning a way of life. Rapid change. New anxieties. Needing distractions or entertainment.

Layers:
Four is the artificial number. Forcing things into artificial order will disappoint. The world can't fit into the boxes we create. It is way too vast for that, thank goodness. Being vast means there are unlimited things to accept. Looking through our limited perception tunnel blocks out so much. What part of the picture are you missing?

With:
5 Cups = depression
Ace wands = feeling uncomfortable with a new situation at work
Ace Coins = feeling uncomfortable with the amount of time effort and energy available to you
Ace Cups = feeling uncomfortable with personal relationships or just unhappy
Other cards can indicate what it is that is making you unhappy.

Five of Cups

Numerical Value: 5

Energy: Clouded perception

Key Words:
Pessimist / Optimist

Divinatory meaning:
Disappointment but opportunity. Is the cup half-full or half-empty? Partial loss. Compromise. Negotiation. Mediation. Union. Espousal. Half way. Re-order and re-evaluate. Turning over a new leaf. Freedom Issues

Ill Dignified:
False starts. Dishonour. Regret. Broken engagements or agreement. Letdowns. Emotional blackmail. Inheritance. Unexpected worries.   Anxieties. Imprisonment.

Layers:
Meet others half way. There is what you desire and what they desire, it doesn't have to be mutually exclusive. You have to give up a little to gain a little. That is the game of life. Single freedom is surrender to the security and perpetuity of the family. There is no use in crying over spilt milk. Your cup is still half full. The two and the three, the yin and the yang, unite in the five.

With:
King Cups = Person who is too emotional.
4 cups = Sadness or depression
King Swords = Need to Compromise
Other cards can indicate what it is you are not happy about.

Six of Cups

Numerical Value: 6

Energy: Past Connections

Key Words:
Reminiscence. Nostalgia. Family gathering.

Divinatory meaning:
The Past. Childhood memories. Old age. Retro style. Former associations bringing present relationships. Good results from past efforts. Pleasant memories. Dreams realised. New elements linked to the past. Past-life connections. Family ties. Sharing memories and values.

Ill Dignified:
Melancholy. Morbidity. Longing. Outdated habits. Old fashioned customs. Exaggerated nostalgia.

Layers:
We live in an eternal now moment. If we turn inward we can see the things we choose to remember or would rather forget. If we turn outward we can see the future as we would like it to be. The present creates the future. The past creates the now. Time is a trick we play on ourselves. Let it go and let it flow.

With:
6 swords = having to travel for friends or family
Sun = Wedding or engagement
4 wands = birthday party
2 cups = meeting a romantic interest at a family gathering or through friends or family.
Devil = Not comfortable at family gatherings or a friend from the past that you would rather not see.
Death = Funeral
Justice = court case
Empress or Ace cups = Birth

Seven of Cups

Numerical Value: 7

Energy: Creative Visionary

Key Words:
The Arts. Creative pursuit. Rose coloured glasses.
Castles in the air.

Divinatory meaning:
Lush. Luxury. Daydreams. Over indulgence. Mystical experience. Inspiration. Too many choices. Opportunities appearing better than they are. Fantasy. Avoid errors of judgement. Be present. Choose carefully this is important spiritually. Excess. Eternal optimist.

Ill Dignified:
Illusions. Delusions. False hopes. Great future plans no present action. Self-delusion. Indecision. From Walter Mity to insanity is a hair's breadth. Fearing success.

Layers:
The future never gets here. "Woulda, Coulda, Shoulda" is the drunken cry of the man who took no action whilst he dreamt. Wishing the future and seeing the reality of possible situations are two different things. Hollywood illusions now make history and rewrite it. By not seeing the goodness of what is the truth the opportunities are lost. This is the watery side of seven's spirituality.

With:
4 or 5 of cups = unfulfilled creative side.
2 cups = see your partner clearly
Lovers = your heart is lyng to you.
9 swords = Worrying over nothing
Page swords = some one trying to manipulate you, see clearly.
Business cards = Check the fine print.

Eight of Cups

Numerical Value: 8

Energy: Move on

Key Words:
Leave what doesn't serve you behind. Time to move.
Free yourself.

Divinatory meaning:
Detachment. Turning point. Cutting ties. Update the
outdated.   Leaving home. Ending a co-dependant
situation. Quitting. Progress. Promotion. Graduation.
Viewpoint Changes. Give up being stubborn. Surrender.

Ill Dignified:
Abandoning security to pursue fantasy. Impossible ideals. Risk.   Restlessness.
Recklessness.

Layers:
Refreshment awaits your soul. Quitting takes strength. Knowing when not to
struggle is wisdom. Discretion is the better part of valour. Tactical retreat
leaves you with strength to carry on elsewhere. Things have gone far enough,
turn and walk away. Refusing to participate in a bad situation is best for others
as well as yourself. Eight is the fullness of all that you can take and give.

With:
2 cups = relationship that no longer serves you
Queen coins = moving house
Ace wands = time to move on to a new job or ask for a pay rise or promotion
Children cards = time to set yourself free by letting them be
6 coins = you are doing too much for others
6 cups = you are not comfortable with your family
4 or 5 cups = staying there is getting you down
10 swords = backstabbing
Kings wands = you are disappearing in a large group
Queens wands = educational institutions not suiting you
King Cups = not happy with your partner
                    Page cups = too idealist for your own good – relax.

Nine of Cups

Numerical Value: 9

Energy: Happiness

Key Words:
Happy Merchant. Content. Success. Heath. Happiness.

Divinatory meaning:
Well-being. Stability. Security. Goodwill. Comfortable circumstances. Planned future. Satisfaction. Plain sailing with work. Liberality. Generosity. Personal YES

Ill Dignified:
Business upsets. Miscalculation. Complacency. Vanity. Self-indulgence. Loss of work ethic. Abuse of hospitality.

Layers:
You achieved your goals for all the right reasons. You provide well and are liked and loved. There is a rose on your cheek, warmth in your heart and well-stocked abundance in all areas of your life. The universe has said "yes" to you. All the gods smile on you and you know just who to call for your needs. Nine is the ennead, the gathering of the gods. It is a blessed and powerful number, brimming over in this case.

With:
6 wands = there is no stopping you on your way to success
9 coins = beautiful life
Business cards = Business does well
Relationship cards = a happy contented life together
Sun = Happy marriage, very blessed
Oracle = Listen to advise from a professional or a trusted friend in order to succeed.

Ten of Cups

Numerical Value: 10

Energy: Personal Fulfilment

Key Words:
Emotional Fulfilment: Happy Endings

Divinatory meaning:
Your blessed. Happiness. Security. Success.   Lasting happy family life. Good reputation. Honour. Friendship. Peace.

Ill Dignified:
 Anti-social actions. Upset routine. Adolescents. Births. Lost friendship. Family quarrels. Disruption.

Layers:
Full filled. Life is everything that you had hoped it would be. You go to bed happy and wake each day with a smile on your lips because life is good. Be wise. Do not take any of this for granted. Give thanks, be appreciative and do what is necessary to head off any upsets. Appreciative people prosper. Those who are ungrateful will slowly have everything taken away from them. Life will still have challenges. Ten is the completion of one cycle. Be ready for the next.

With:
Most cards will indicate what you are enjoying
10 Coins = happiness and security
9 cups or coins = You know how things should be, you are nearly there.
2 cups or Ace cups = happy relationship
King cups = a partner who understand you
Work or business card = Job satisfaction
6 coins, knight cups = loving helping others

Page of Cups
Female Energy under 40
Water
Young Wounded Idealist

Energy: New Romantic

Element: Earth of Water

Key Words:
The 'out of breath' activist. Do not allow yourself to be taken advantage of by others.

Personality Type: Princess Diana

Divinatory meaning:
Loyal idealist. Starting point. Imagination. Good news. Engagement. Marriage. Birth. Kind. Gentle. Reflective. Poetic. Quiet. Artistic. Foresight. A jack-of-all-trades. Desire for starting a family. Inexperience.

Ill Dignified:
Don't let others take advantage of your better nature. Self-deception. Shallow. Non-committal. Scheming. Aesthetic but not artistic. Secretive. Lies. Slander.

Layers:
What new things could this Page spread in the world to do good with tireless enthusiasm for assisting others. The wounded healer knows where the pain lays yet still sees the joy and the miracle of the world. So much to be done, we had better start now.

With:
6 coins = doing too much for others
Knight cups = a good partner or personal relationship - functioning from the same ideals
9 wands = exercise caution or get some one to watch out for you.
Other cards will indicate what areas in which to protect yourself

Knight of Cups
Male Energy Under 40
Water
The Activist

MAHATMA GHANDI
ROMANTIC IDEALIST

Energy: Romantic Idealist

Element: Fire of Water

Key Words:
Liking things just so. Perfectionist. Being admired for what you are. Bringing you words of love. A proposal. Solutions.

Personality Type: Gandhi

Divinatory meaning:
Poetic soul. Spiritual opportunity. Change. Excitements. Romance. Invitations. Opportunities. Bringer of ideas or words of love. Refined. Poet. Artist. Singer. Empathetic. Feeling the pain of others. Amiable. Intelligent. High principals. Dreamer. Easily discouraged.

Ill Dignified:
Lot of ideas but few capabilities. Unfinished symphonies. Quests begun then abandoned and forgotten. Unreliable. Recklessness. False promises. Congenital liar. Deceives self as well as others.

Layer:
The bringer of heart soul and solution. This knight is questing to prove himself to himself. He offers the cup that inspires solution. Melancholy, he misses the mark of his too high ideals yet gets to the heart of the matter.

With:
Page cups = Good match
5 wands = Pushing yourself too hard – learn to compromise
Knight swords = Don't react impulsively
Queen swords = Pick your moment to achieve you best result
3 swords = Don't hurt yourself trying to help others
6 coins – Doing too much for others

Queen of Cups
Feminine Energy over 40
Water
The Beloved

Energy: Object of Romance

Element: Water of Water

Key Words:
Allow yourself to be loved. Know that you are loved.
Let yourself see how many do love you.

Personality Type: Marilyn Monroe

Divinatory meaning:
Tender. Dreamy. This person is loved and creates an otherworldly atmosphere around them. Psychic. Stylish. Balance. Harmony. Over sensitive. Imaginative. Artistic. Affectionate. Romantic. Easily influenced by people, events, and environments. Lack of common sense, yet heightened intuition. Handle things gently.

Ill Dignified:
Petulance. Ingratitude. Spoilt. Fickleness. Unreliable. Changeable. Unstable. Hysterical. They may even lead others to destruction in pursuit of a fantasy.

Layers:
You will be loved despite yourself, when it is least wanted. People impute their emotions to you. This queen gently commands adoration. You feel so much.

With:
King cups = an emotional partner
Knight cups = an admirer
2 cups = romance
Lovers = unfaithfulness
8 cups = time to move on in relationships
Queen swords = pick you moments
4 coins = be the emotional miser
Any 5s = situation improving

King for Cups
Male EnergyOver 40
Water
The Lover

Element: Air of Water

Energy: Poignant

Key Words:
Melancholy, big hearted lover. Emotional

Personality Type: Orpheus

Divinatory meaning:
Admired. Loving but often not loved. Respected. Considerate. Responsible. Kind. Romantic. Skilled negotiator. Well connected. Caring. Reliability. Mature. Solitary. Shy. Covert. Secretive. Psychotherapist. Counsellor. Priest. Artist. Musician. Philosopher. Self-Control.

Ill Dignified:
Narcissist. Hedonist. Amoral.　Self-centred.　Sociopath. Scandal. Vice. Corruption. Toying with others. Abusive.

Layers:
Lovingly tender, he's known pain and has great empathy. Singing the lament. "Don't look back, you can never look back," he always looks back longing for what was lost. His great love is gone forever. Having given his heart away there it stays, beyond hope. King of the art of love if not its practicalities. This is a man who loves people.

With:
10 cups = happy relationship
9 cups = success, health and happiness improving for this individual.
2 cups = a very romantic lover
4 or 5 cups = An emotional person whose moods can go up and down.
5 coins = emotional situation has gone as far as it will go - improving now
Court cards will tell you more about this romantic interest.
7 cups = a musical/creative person

The Suit

of

Swords

The Suit of Swords

Ace of Swords
Element of Fire

Numerical Value: 1

Season: Summer

Direction: North

Energy: Start something

Key Words:
Impetus. Impulsiveness, Passion.

Divinatory meaning:
Passion. Drive. Protection. Ambition. Enthusiasm. A boy. Impulsiveness.
Aggressive pursuit of ventures. Male. Authority. Triumph. Victory. Success.
Insemination.

Ill Dignified:
Indolent. Misuse of power. Can answer questions on death, via surrounding
cards. Trouble with men in a woman's spread. Thuggery. Violence. Destruction.

Layer:
The father protects his family and clan. Shoulder to shoulder with his mates he
will stand. The male will sacrifice himself for the female and strives to bring
her what she needs. The sword is the implement of directed will. This ace is
about directing it in better ways.

With:
Other cards will reveal what you are being or need to be focused on.
With any of the fertility or birth cards can indicate a male baby
Business cards = New business drive
Health cards = Health improving
7 cups = The focus on new creative concepts
Ace wands = Determination to start new job
Ace coins = New venture brings new money
Ace cups = Determined to be happy
Death = Death

Two of Swords

2 TWO OF SWORDS

CAMARADERIE, FRIENDSHIP
TENSE BALANCE, TRUCE 2

Numerical Value: 2

Energy: Choices

Key Words:
Tense balance. Strong partnerships. Rally good friendships. Camaraderie.
Getting the backup that you need.

Divinatory meaning:
Delicate balance.   Allies. Decide carefully. Courage. Differences resolved. Truce. Point of power. Middle way.

Ill Dignified:
Razors edge. Imbalance. Stress. Tension. Deception. Misleading advice. Betrayal. Be brave make your choice.

Layers:
The dyad, about partnerships and polarities, is here held equal. This strong force that can only exist between pairs. Stasis hangs in the balance. The pivot point allows mobility and leverage. Inertia outweighs gravity. Impartial to which rises or falls, the middle cares not for the polar opposites, yet cannot exists without them. Though opposing, they are two of a kind, sharpening and strengthening each other. Formidable sister battleships are like strong partnerships. Steel sharpens steel.

With:
2 wands = team work
3 cups = networking
Justice = it could go either way
2 cups = a friendship could be come romantic
6 coins = helping someone who appreciates it.

Three of Swords

3 THREE OF SWORDS

NEW ACTION DISOLVES OLD
CONFLICT; HEARTBREAK **3**

Numerical Value: 3

Energy: Pain

Key Words:
Cut away the pain. Leave you pain in the past - don't repeat it.

Divinatory meaning:
Stop hurting yourself. Move away from pain. Just do it. Effort needed. New energy. Third partner. Establishment of something better. Getting serious. Learning to direct your will. Put your heart into it. Join in.

Ill Dignified:
Sorrow. Heartache. Lack. Loneliness. Team disharmony. Confusion. Breaking a truce. Enmity. Physical disorder. Internal conflict. Jealous partners. Self-restriction.

Layers:
Equal to the depth of sorrows there will be the heights of joy. It is easy to blame others for discomfort. But why let this in to where it could wound you? The pain in this three can be an initiation opening your eyes. There are others in your life that backs you up. Where do you want to go? Allow those who strengthen you help to get you there. Triads are three-strand cords not easily broken.

With:
Other cards will reveal where your pain lies.
9 swords = worrying about past pain.
10 swords = someone trying to cause you pain
8 swords or devil = Needing to move away from a painful situation
4 or 5 cups = see what you do have instead of wanting what you don't.

Four of Swords

Numerical Value: 4

Energy: Non-action

Key Words:
Complete Rest

Divinatory meaning:
Retreat. Withdrawal. Breath deep, seek peace. Rest. Recovery. Recuperation Responsible Actions. Relief from anxiety or sorrow. Sabbatical. Take time out for you

Ill Dignified:
Depression. Discrimination. Enforced isolation. Hospitalisation. Seclusion. Imprisonment. Cowardice.

Layers:
Muscle builds organically not under the artificial contrivance of the four. There is a time to stop pushing. This is the biggest lesson when learning to wield the will. The sword energy of creating the world according to your will requires great effort and sometimes you must rest. Doing nothing allows your energy to regroup, your wounds to heal, and your body to become stronger. In Asia the word for 'four' is 'Shi' this is also the word for 'death'. Stop what you are doing. Desist. Have a break.

With:
Other cards will reveal what you need a rest from.
6 swords = short distance holiday
8 wands = long distance holiday.

Five of Swords

Numerical Value: 5

Energy: Cunning

Key Words:
Disarming skill and astuteness. Executing the plan. Doing what is necessary to get the job done. Steering around likely problems.

Divinatory meaning:
Strategy. Common sense. Disarming shrewdness.

Ill Dignified:
Surgery. Defeat. Failure. Dishonour. Break-free. Belligerence. Humbling. Harassment. Inaction. Malice. Spite.

Layers:
Common sense is no longer common. A fight can be over before it has begun by disarming your opponent. Conflict is pushing against the other in brute strength. Leaving nothing to push against, nowhere to fight, nor anything to fight with, makes you a winner. The dinosaurs became smaller whilst the alpha-males were challenging each other, leaving the non-threatening males alone to impregnate the females. De-evolve the argument. Fives are about self-replicating cycles. You can choose to break the conflict cycle if you are shrewd. Cunning is a spiritual quality, being a doormat isn't.

With:
9 wands = heading off problems
7 wands = easily done with planning
Business cards = business planning
Love cards = playing smart in a relationship so that it fulfils your needs
10 swords = look deeper into others motivations towards you
Devil = plans not working
2 swords = wait - plans not working yet
Emperor or 4 coins = check you figures before you proceed

Six of Swords

Numerical Value: 6

Energy: Shifting

Key Words:
Obligations. Travel for others

Divinatory meaning:
Feeling stuck but having to move. Travel away form difficulty. Short journeys. Needing or giving assistance. You need your friends. Family steps in. Family or work calls, you go. Witness.

Ill Dignified:
Unplanned travel. Relatives or friends need you. Need for continuing effort and strength for others. Limitations.

Layers:
Being called we answer. Moving through life is not always where we want to go. Acting for others can sometimes move us further than we will move ourselves. Taking them aid, assistance or strengthening their will. Adding your will to justice you step forward for others. This heptad's energy is about the balanced forces of justice, helping to even things out and doing what you feel is the right thing to do.

With:
6 cups = travelling for a family get together
Work or business cards = travelling for work
Love cards = long distance relationship
4 swords = needing to get away

Seven of Swords

Numerical Value: 7

Energy: Stealth

Key Words:
Sly prevention. Heading off conflict before it begins is the ultimate form of martial arts.

Divinatory meaning:
Stealing the advantage. Liberation. Determination. Spirit is on your side. Daring. Self-defence. Prevention. Pre-emptive action. Foresight. Change of residence/job. Triumph through cunning.

Ill Dignified:
No real progress. Lack of purpose. Reluctance.   Surrender when victory is almost in sight. Follow through.

Layers:
You have to remove the ammunition before it can be used against you. The Spartans stole the only advantage they had to protect their nation even though they were prohibited by law. Stealth can be a protection for you and your loved ones. Being a seven shows that stealth, like cunning, can serve a higher spiritual purpose. A stitch in time saves nine. Prevention is better than cure.

With:
Business cards = formulating a business plan
Page swords = manipulating the manipulators
5 swords = conflict prevention
9 wands = self protection.
Queens coins = home security
Page wands = good study habits

Eight of Swords

Numerical Value: 8

Energy: Courage

Key Words:
Feeling stuck. Be bold step forward

Divinatory meaning:
Restriction. Wanting to move. Feeling fearful / bogged down. Don't be afraid. Holding yourself back. Action is needed. A new goal but not knowing how to achieve it.

Ill Dignified:
Crisis. Oppression. Hard work. Stuck. Trapped. Contractual obligations. Action not possible.

Layers:
Babies feel restricted before they leave the womb then cry, feeling cold and not comforted. Teenagers feel cramped before they leave home seeking independence, then keep asking for assistance to cope with the new found freedom and responsibility. Restriction prompts growth but it is a two edged sword. Fleeing restriction we exchange one discomfort for another. Eight is expansion. The process of enlarging ourselves to fit into a bigger space leaves us floundering in vast unfamiliarity.

With:
Other cards will reveal where the energy is stuck - free it up

Nine of Swords

Numerical Value: 9

Energy: Turmoil

Key Words:
Worries. Sleepless nights. Get out of the house.

Divinatory meaning:
Accept help. Find peace. Get vindication. It will all work out OK. No worries mate!

Ill Dignified:
Depression. Disruption. Disturbances. Don't play the martyr. Premonitions. Bad dreams. Suffering. Cruelty. Disappointment. Loss. Scandal. Paranoia. Tears.

Layers:
The points of all that worries you keep raking through your mind. Your stomach churns. Panic attacks pound your heart. The points become a bed of nails on which you cannot relax. Your dreams are torn on an uncertain future. Nine is the near completion. You do not wish to continue down this path to its ultimate conclusion. A drastic change is needed immediately. If no action can be taken then be gentle with yourself and let your poor wounded heart rest. Sleep knits the ragged ends of care.

With:
9 cups = worrying that things are to good or worrying about your health.
Other cards will reveal what you are worried about

Ten of Swords

Numerical Value: 10

Energy: Completion

Key Words:
It can't get any worse! Someone has the knives out for you, beware.

Divinatory meaning:
Its all over! The lowest point in the cycle, from now on things can only get better. The worst is over. Successful endings or journeys

Ill Dignified:
Pain. Dramatic endings. Lifting of burdens. Release from afflictions. Sudden extreme change. Violence.

Layers:
There is no fixing this. It has run its course. Pinned down. This can't go on anymore. Let go. It is finished. Release what has been dammed up as this water belongs in the ocean. To keep trying will only hurt you more. Go no further. Don't do violence to yourself. Move away from the thing causing you pain, quickly. It's dead, let it be. Ten means the cycle has concluded. Look to starting something new.

With:
Page swords = Mal-intended covert manipulation
Justice = Watch you back
Temperance = change the people or thing in your life that prevent you form being stronger.
Court cards can give you more information about who it is.

Page of Swords
Feminine Energy Under 40
Fire
Sudden Beginnings

Element: Earth of Fire

Energy: New Protective

Key Words:
Trying something new.

Personality Type: Margaret Thatcher

Divinatory meaning:
Starting point. Forceful. Patience. Attached. Impetuous. A trustworthy, reliable young person. A petty manipulative older person. Excitement. Grace and dexterity. Spying. Surveying others. Cunning.

Ill Dignified:
Belligerent. Vindictive. Searching for hidden weaknesses. Devious. Snooping in other people's business. Unforeseen events. Ill health. Chaotic.

Layers:
When something needs doing this person won't wait for the possibility of someone else coming forward, they are the first one to jump in boots and all. They can appear to be the individual least likely. Pages are the beginnings of this energy appearing in a person. This can be new impetus, energy, or action in a stagnant stalemate.

With:
9 wands = some who believes that are trying to protect you even though that may not be what you want
6 cups = family manipulation
Work cards = manipulation at work.
Personal relationship = personal manipulation
Court cards can real more about this person

Knight of Swords
Male Energy Under 40
Fire
Action Hero

Energy: Reactive Proactive

Element: Fire of Fire

Key Words:
Charging in. Impulsiveness. Aggressive Movement.
Action Man. Protective. Reactive. Challenges.

Personality Type: Guy Fawkes

Divinatory meaning:
The archetypal warrior. Action lover. Forceful. Strong. Always arriving or departing. Courageous. Someone who is well liked, energetic, confident, but sometimes unpredictable. Thrives on difficult situations. Dominant.

Ill Dignified:
Impetuous. Upstart. Berserk. Over-reaction. Noncommittal. Quarrels. Indulgence.

Layers:
This is the original action hero who makes Hollywood hard men look like prissy gigolos. Errol Flynn would give anything just to be like this one. Indiana Jones looks a bit pointless and insipid next to this energy, as there is always a greater purpose to this card. However, knights are the action of that element and this one can be hotly passionate then rapidly changeable, impulsive and fickle.

With:
Other cards csn show you where you impulsiveness lays and if this is good or bad for you
5 wands = Loving the challenge
7 wands = easily over coming challenges
9 wands = very protective
Fool = don't rush in
5 or 7 swords = plan before you act
Other court cards can show who you have a reaction too.

Queen of Swords
Female Energy Over 40
Fire
The Defender

Energy: Maternal Protective

Element: Water of Fire

Key Words:
Timing. Bight your tongue and bide your time. Hell hath no fury. Ice queen until it is time to act then a blaze of fiery action.

Personality Type: St Joan of Arc

Divinatory meaning:
Be the ice queen not the hot head. Complex. Feisty. Fiery. Courageous. Justice. Patience. Woman who has overcome adversity from men. Capability. Talented. Protective towards her circle. Nurture your actions.

Ill Dignified:
Impulsive. Jealous. Reactive. Impatience. Brash. Loss of passion. Victim. Possessive. Loss of passion. A formidable enemy.

Layers:
The passionate woman, exhilarating, fierce and pointedly focused. A doe, when seized by this energy, can kick the wolf to death that threatens her young. Pity the Roman soldier that Queen Bodicea found assaulting her daughters. Her fury destroyed 20 legions, briefly liberating England. Kali Ma with planning. Joan's well-timed frenzied visions freed France. Eleanor of Aquitaine. Elizabeth 1st of England.

With:
Queen cups = Don't let you needs out weigh your wants
Ace cups = Timing is needed to bring you fulfilment.
4 or 5 swords = Good timing with your plans will make you unstoppable.
2 swords = Wait. Not yet. You may need backup
        Other cards can indicate in what areas you need to have good timing.

King of Swords
Male Energy Over 40
Fire
The Leader

Energy: Dominant Protective

Element: Air of Fire

Key Words:
Authority Figures. Conflict of intentions. Power Struggles.
Controlling situation or person.

Personality Type: Leonidas of Sparta

Divinatory meaning:
Passionate Control. Advocate of law and order. Non-traditional. Loves home and family life. Passionate. Virile. Moral support. Encouragement. Ruler. Alert. Act without hesitation. Do not provoke. Control your actions

Ill Dignified:
Drama-queen King. Challenges authority. Disruptive. Controlling. Ignoble. Repugnant. Distain for weakness. Abuse of power/authority. Obstinate. Vicious. Vigilanté.

Layers:
The God Mars was a protective family man, appointed patron of Rome because he was more tender to his children than Zeus. Leonidas defied the Gods to protect his home, paying the ultimate price without hesitation. This king is an authority figure that has more heart than the King of Wands but can be fiery and stubborn with their point of view. This can result in power and conflict issues.

With:
Queen cups = Protective about their love. Needing to be loved.
2 swords = Loyal friendships. Strong teamwork.
Hermit = Isolated by authority.
4 or 5 Cups = Need to compromise.
Knight cups = Unlikely to compromise.
9 cups = You are doing this for the right reasons, you will succeed.
Other court cards can show whom you may have conflicting agendas with and the minor arcana cards will show why

The Suit

of

Pentacles

The Suit of Pentacles

Ace of Pentacles
Element of Earth

Numerical Value: 1

Season: Winter

Direction: South

Energy: New cycle

Key Words: Upsurge in time, effort, energy and money available to you or a project

Divinatory meaning:
Financial betterment. New house, car or thing. Prosperity. Family. Abundance. Material comfort with time, effort and energy. We don't just spend money. Good health. Appreciation. Nuts and bolts of day-to-day living. Windfall. Gift. Settling Down. End to travelling.

Ill Dignified:
Greed, Hedonism. Miserliness, Materialism. Lack of imagination and fear of death. Selfishness.

Layers:
The wheel turns and the only thing that is constant in life is change... till now. This cycle is the beginning of what you truly want from material life. The monad signals that there is an upsurge in energy is available to you to accomplish this. This may be done quietly. However, you will feel more contented.

With:
Other cards will reveal what material areas will improve for you.
With any of the fertility or birth cards, can indicate a female baby
Business cards = Doing well in business
Health cards = Health improving
7 cups = The need to be practical, realistic and very down to earth
Ace wands = Home based business or enough form you work to live comfortably
Ace cups or 10 cups = Happiness and contentment at home
Ace swords = Home and home life are your focus

Two of Pentacles

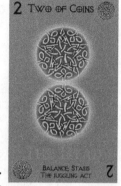

Numerical Value: 2

Energy: Commitment

Key Words:
Keep things in balance. A Juggling act. The money go round. It is flowing in and going out but not building up.

Divinatory meaning:
Juggling life situations. Financial commitments. Change. Movement. Negotiation. Preparation. Contracts. Agreements. Skilful Navigation. Handling business.

Ill Dignified:
Recklessness. Listen to warnings. Debt. Over-indulgence. Unfinished symphonies.

Layers:
It is hard to keeping all of your balls in the air. Constant effort is required. The moment we stop it all falls down. With the material world comes pleasures but pleasures bring responsibilities. Smiling we begin the financial game. The dyad shows us the way through this is balance. The power is again in the middle way. Don't go to financial extremes or stretch yourself out too far. Play it close to your chest and keep your bases covered.

With:
Justice = Life balancing out
Hanged Man = No forward movement
3 cups = trying to juggle work and social responsibilities
6 cups, swords or coins = trying to balance family responsibilities with the rest of your life
6 wands, 9 cups 9 coins, 10 cups, 10 coins = you will win long term.
Other cards will indicate what areas you are trying to balance.

Three of Pentacles

Numerical Value: 3

Energy: Business

Key Words:
Golden opportunity. Apprenticeships. New opportunity. Initiations.

Divinatory meaning:
Rewards. Recognition. Successful sale. New business dealings. New skills. Successful beginnings. Fun Job. Enjoying work. Financial increase.   Craftsman. Merchant.   Rewards. Appreciated.   New project. Help in business. 1st initiation.

Ill Dignified:
Missed opportunities. Not accepting advice. Obstinacy. Conceit. Prejudice. Disappointing results.

Layers:
You have been accepted in but now the real works starts. Its new, there's potential and it is where you want to go. You are excited but there's a lot to learn, new rules, new etiquette, new skills and new levels to play upon. This is what you want to do for yourself but you have to work in with others. Triads are new initiations and teamwork.

With:
3 wands = Wow! Fantastic new opportunities
Any 5s = Getting better from here.
Queen swords = don't miss this opportunity
Sun = YES!
Ace wands = New work opportunity.

Four of Pentacles

Numerical Value: 4

Energy: Material responsibility

Key Words:
The Wise Miser. Budgeting your time, effort, energy and money.

Divinatory meaning:
Watch your pennies. Haggling. Material security. Influential. Promotion. Negotiation. Delegate work. Stock markets. Banks. Building your finances.

Ill Dignified:
Micro-management. Bureaucracy. Greed. A fear of loss. Opposition to change. Insecurity.

Layers:
Being careful where you spend your energy and time is wise. Money is only one form of energy. Who and what are absolutely necessary? Humans and their organisations will drain you if you let them. Their artificial constructs are set up for a purpose, but is it your purpose? Use them where necessary, wisely. The tetrad in the earth element is about man-made financial institutions not fair exchange and remuneration

With:
5 coins = Things have been tough – be tough on your self to make it better
Fool = Penny wise and pound foolish
Knight Swords = Beware impulse purchases
6 coins or page cups or knight cups = Withdraw your energy from others
7 wands = You can do it – if you do what needs to be done
Pages swords = Have less to do with manipulative people
4 swords = You need some you time
King cups = Pull your energy back from your partner
2 cups = Proceed slowly

Five of Pentacles

Numerical Value: 5

Energy: Subsistence

Key Words:
Pushed to the limit. Stretched thin on time, effort, energy, and money. Stressed

Divinatory meaning:
Patterns and behaviours around money and material things need work. Financially tight. You've been through the worst. Things will start to improve. Restrictions may open doors in ways you haven't previously considered.

Ill Dignified:
Don't be despondent. Redundancy. Financial loss. Material worries. Poverty-consciousness. Lack of success. Lack of imagination. Narrow mindedness. Lack of foresight. The ant and the grasshopper.

Layers:
Thank goodness that you have been through the wost of things. Improvement happens if you have learnt the lessons and don't repeat the patterns. Material things are as pliable to your will as any other form of energy. Energy is work. This pentad reveals what your efforts reproduce.

With:
5 Cups = you have been pushed to your lowest ebb. The only way is up. Don't be afraid to ask for help.
Tower = Sudden bad turn of events.
Other cards will tell you what energies that you have pushed to the limit.

Six of Pentacles

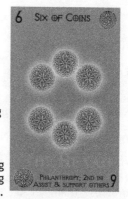

Numerical Value: 6

Energy: Sharing

Key Words:
Philanthropy. Helping others. Chronic helper. Repaying debts.

Divinatory meaning:
Selfless charitable work. Receiving loans. Helping family. Clearance of debts. Good fortune, benefiting others. Repayment of favours. Charity. Patronage. Sympathy. Kindness.

Ill Dignified:
Over generous. Thoughtless. Careless with money. Deceit. Extravagance. Someone else's problem. Not my circus not my monkey.

Layers:
The measure of wealth is not how much money you have but having enough left over to help others. Charity begins at home. It's easier to give money to family rather than what they really need. Preventing and fixing problems takes so much more. This hexad is balance of earthy elements. The place between tough love and smother. The energy of giving to family has many forms. Subsistence, praise, comfort, support, and attention. Practise on them before attempting to assist others.

With:
6 cups = Family needing help
2 swords = friends needing help
2 wands work mates needing help
3 cups = acquaintances wanting help
4 coins = Do less - withdraw your energy
Money cards = Financial assistance
4 or 5 cups = Emotional support
Page or Knight cups = Charity work or causes
Other court cards can indicate which person around you is wanting/needing assistance

Seven of Pentacles

Numerical Value: 7

Energy: Stock Take

Key Words:
Sowing the seeds of your future. Persistence. Fruition.

Divinatory meaning:
You don't plant tomato seeds toady and pick tomatoes tomorrow. Patience. Endurance. Nearing Payoff. About to reap the rewards for your hard work. Review your progress then get on with things again. The quiet achiever. Unnoticed success. Keep up the hard work - your nearly there! Working hard without correct remuneration.

Ill Dignified:
What's the point? Pushing too hard. Giving up too soon. Promising circumstances that end in failure.   Unobservant. Inertia. Not worthy the effort. Laziness. Unappreciated effort.

Layers:
You are at a crossroads but don't deviate. What you have worked so hard for is about to occur. You can't see an end in sight but it is bursting into life around you. You have planned and directed your energies well. It is nearly here. The heptad is the spiritual side of earthy things. What you wished for is manifesting in the real world.

With:
5 or 7 swords = Acting on plans made.
Career cards = Starting to move into the right career path for you.
Family Cards = Starting to move into the right direction for your family.
7 cups = Make sure that you actions are practical.
Lovers = More than one thing that you can do.

Eight of Pentacles

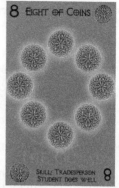

Numerical Value: 8

Energy: Physical Progress

Key Words:
Mastering skills that bring a new stream of income. End of study/apprenticeship and the beginning of career.

Divinatory meaning:
Working hard. Close to completing an apprenticeship or course of study. Profitable skills. Increase in available money. Annuity etc. matures. Talented. Enthusiastic. Continued success through attention to the details. Doing a great job.

Ill Dignified:
Craftiness. Dishonesty. Inappropriate use of energy and skills. Sly business affairs. Short-term gain at the expense of long-term profit.

Layers:
You are mastering the world around you. Things are going well. You have focused your energies into the things that serve you the best and it has rewarded you. This octad is about expansion. Zeus, the god of the expansive sky, blesses you. Things are looking very bright for you. Craft and skill have moved into the art form. Continue working well. Laugh and be happy.

With:
Page wands = Making money from what you have learned.
Queen coins or 8 cups = Sale/rental of assets.
4 coins = Wise investments.
Ace wands = New job.
2 cups or Sun = Marrying well.
7 cups = Money from creative or artistic pursuits.

Nine of Pentacles

9 NINE OF COINS

AESTHETICS; TRANQUILITY
ORDER FROM CHAOS 6

Numerical Value: 9

Energy: Order from chaos

Key Words:
Beauty. Balance. Perfection. Harmony. Placement.
Aesthetics. Rewards and wins

Divinatory meaning:
Positioning. The right place at the right time. The
enjoyment. Humanitarian. Mentoring. Peace. Beauty.
Tranquillity. Financial gains. Gifts. Winnings.
Inheritances. Settlements. Popularity. Common sense. Organised.

Ill Dignified:
Affluence. Ill mannered. Swindling. Con artists. The lull before the storm.

Layers:
Placement creates beauty. This is the basis of FengSui. Creating beauty and
natural flow is the basis of living in harmony. The more we flow with the larger
picture of the nine planets and the nine gods the easier our life becomes.
Position, position, position, creates value in more things than real estate.
Value beauty and harmony results in ease in your life. En-joy.

With:
Queen swords = Perfect timing
9 cups = Things going very well. An unbeatable combination
10 cups, Sun, Star, or World = you are very blessed.
Queen coins = you have a sense of how life should be and you will not quit
until you achieve this.

Ten of Pentacles

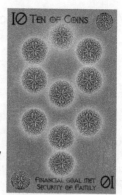

Numerical Value: 10

Energy: Finalising Things

Key Words:
Stability and security of family and finances

Divinatory meaning:
Emotional stability. Safety.   Happiness. Family fortunes. Inheritance. Family traditions.   Goodwill. Settlements and Closure. Affluence. End of a cycle

Ill Dignified:
The will being read. Affluenza.   Family arguments about money. Estate settlement. Burglary.

Layers:
The tree has sprouted strong branches and put down solid roots. The Tree of Life can be the family tree, with its roots in the underworld and its top in the heavens. Your world rotates around it. Great peace contentment and harmony is there. Life is good and you are happy. The gift of your DNA, symbolised by The World Tree has spread further in this world than you thought possible. The energy of the material has reached its happiest and fullest. You're Blessed.

With:
10 cups = happy contented family life.
3 cups or 3 coins = New opportunity doing very well.
Ace coins = Windfall
5 or 7 swords = Financial planning
Oracle = Wise professional advice works well for you financially
Justice = Profiting from a court case or settlement.

Page of Pentacles
Female Energy under 40
Earth
The Enthusiast

Energy: New Achiever

Element: Earth of Earth

Key Words:
Setting new long term goals.
Acquisitions of things or skills needed for the success of a plan.

Personality Type: Bill Gates

Divinatory meaning:
Conceptual starting point. Child of Earth. Dogged. Meticulous. Hardworking. Administrator. Diligent. A plan is needed. Set goals and plan your approach. Impish. News about business, health or home. Crystals. Gems.

Ill Dignified:
Overzealous. No sense of humour. Impractical. Autocratic. Unwelcome financial news.

Layers:
Studious planning proceeds successful action. Consumed to a one pointedness. Doggedly loyal unless friends turn fowl then the student will overtake the former masters, becoming a greater master and eclipsing them. Pages are news and this news is good. What newly starts here surly takes over. The beginning of the rise and rise and rise in the material world.

With:
Other cards will indicate what long-term goals are being made or need to be made.

Knight of Pentacles
Male Energy Under 40
Earth
The Strategist

Energy: Practical Achievement

Element: Fire of Earth

Key Words:
No risks. Strategy. Action only when the plan shows success.
Only enter the battle field when you know that the battle is already won.

Personality Type: Gengis Khan

Divinatory meaning:
Movement. Steady progress. Traditional. Family oriented. Financial planning. Patient. Waits for the perfect opportunity then acts quickly. Hardworking. Slow and steady progress. The earth is slow but the oxen are patient.

Ill Dignified:
Greedy. Grasping person. Smug. Impassive. Indifferent. Stoic. Unappreciative. Insensitive. Financial standstill.

Layer:
Do not react. Wait. Plan your tactic. Re-action gives away your control. Don't be steered by others. Knights are action, but here stands still and waits for the absolute right moment. The Mongols brought the code of chivalry and the concept of the mounted warrior to the west.

With:
9 wands = take your time and be very cautious.
Page swords = Do not let others push you into things before you are ready.
King Wands = Like structured ordered environments where others take responsibility.
Knight swords = A call to action but move steadily - don't rush.
Queen swords = Wait for the perfect moment.
6 swords = You have to act now.
Business cards = Take no risk in business ventures.
Relationship cards = Take no risk in Relationships

Queen Of Pentacles
Female Energy Over 40
Earth
The Nurturer

Energy: Practical Mother

Element: Water of Earth

Key Words:
Home is my castle/empire. House.
Renovations. Earth Mother.
Provides comfort for those around her and self

Personality Type: Queen Victoria

Divinatory meaning:
Capable. Practical. Loyal.   Businessperson. Material comforts. Responsible.
Tight inner circle. Depth of feeling. Appreciative. Pleasures. Luxuries. Routine.
Home or business is the domain.

Ill Dignified:
Impractical. Superficial. Materialistic. Sycophantic. Dogmatic. Narrow-minded.
Misunderstanding. Extravagance. Upset routine.

Layers:
Comforting others requires strength. Tidy spaces relax people, pedantic ones
hold tension. Walking with kings and not loosing the common touch is inner
confidence. Supplying the needs of others requires recognising them. This
queen walks as the earth mother and the empress.

With:
8 wands or 6 swords = moving home.
7 coins = renovations.
10 cups = Happy home.
9 cups = Working to provide something for the home.
9 coins = Everything just so.
4 or 5 coins = Something's not right at home.
5 or 7 swords = planning the perfect environment.
Business cards = work environment.

King of Pentacles
Mature Male Energy
Earth
Dominant Feminine

Energy: Dominant Achiever

Element: Air of Earth

Key Words:
Long term Goals Achieved. Success of a plan.
Structure. Organisations.

Personality Type: Julius Caesar

Divinatory meaning:
Take control. Get busy. A loyal and dependable leader. Trustworthy. Patient as long as things are done their way. Cautious. Wise. Wealthy. Long-suffering. Ritual. Routine. Get hands on.

Ill Dignified:
Rigid. Bribery. Dull. Materialistic. Mercenary. Blinkered. Hates change. Inflexible.

Layer:
Success is achieved through practical attention to details that most others don't see as important. Happy assisting those within his circle, there must be some advantage to assisting those not close. A father figure, a good boss or mentor. This achiever functions best in highly structured environments yet creates structure wherever he is.

With:
Other cards denote where the success lays and what long tem plans are realised.

Afterword

This final section, following, is a special dedication to the late, great, Giorgio Tavaglione whose artwork inspired my own. His depth and breath of knowledge about the Tarot and its correspondences and connections to my ancestors (Sforzas) will be sorely missed. Blessings on your journey through the Summerland's.

The Author's Personal Tarot Connections

The Visconti-Sforza deck is the oldest European Tarot, so Tavaglione, like Coleman-Smith, went directly to the source to derive many of his images. Leonardo Da Vinci's "Lady With an Ermine" is from the same place and time but now rests in The Czartoryskich Museum, Krakow. Coincidentally, her portrait underwent extreme repainting during "The Bonfires of the Vanities" period, in order to save it from destruction. What mystic symbolism in the background of this portrait could have been so offensive to the church as to require that it be over-painted with black? Additionally, there is a vague similarity between the face of the woman in the portrait and the pregnant 'Popess' card of the Sforza Tarocchi, in whose hand rests a deck of cards instead of an ermine.

The author above at the same age as Cecilia in the Da Vinci portrait to the left

Leonardo's portrait depicts Cecilia Gallerani, the favourite and most celebrated of the many mistresses of Ludovico Sforza, known as Lodovico il Moro, Duke of Milan whom Leonardo served. While Leonardo was working as an aspiring court engineer/artist, Cecilia posed for the painting. Young Cecilia was a patron of the arts and a tarot reader. At an early age Cecilia was recognised as a gifted poet, musician, and songstress. She spoke fluent Latin and became hostess of the first "Salon" in Europe, she herself presiding over the philosophical round table discussions. She invited Leonardo to these meetings of elite Milanese philosophers, intellectuals and Masons who encouraged opposition to the Papacy. Therefore, It is not surprising that she may have become the model for card 2, the 'High Priestess' in that original deck. Yet there is a better candidate, predating her, supported by the research of Tarot historians, such as Michael Dummett in his book "*The Visconti-Sforza Tarot Cards.*"

The Hidden Line of Female Popes & The Real Da Vinci Code

The Papess card has been a mysterious and disturbing force, spreading anxiety instead of the calm assurance one might expect from The Faith. The European version of this archetype is based upon Popess Manfreda, of the Guglielmite order of Lombard, a relative of the Visconti family, who has other family members depicted in the tarot cards painted by Bonifacio Bembo.

The Guglielmites thought that Guglielma would descend from heaven to earth in 1300 to inaugurate a line of Popesses to replace the male Popes. Maifreda Visconti da Pirovano was to be declared Pope in a Mass in the Church of Santa Maria Maggiore on Easter 1300, ushering in a new age of the Holy Spirit. Instead, Maifreda and others in the sect were, that year, burned at the stake, along with the disinterred body of Guglielma, who had inspired this new movement. The sect was exterminated by the Inquisition.

The sect had an interesting social life in which there was equality of the genders. There was no emphasis on virginity in the sect, though a good number of the female members were widowed or unmarried. What is interesting, is that the members of the sect crossed social boundaries. There were very wealthy people involved as well as poor servants.

Gertrude Moakley writes:

> "Their leader, Guglielma of Bohemia, had died in Milan in 1281. The most enthusiastic of her followers believed that she was the incarnation of the Holy Spirit, sent to inaugurate the new age of the Spirit prophesied by Joachim of Flora."

Visconti-Sforza Popess/Priestess card. Her Papal cross at top left is hard to see.

They believed that Guglielma would return to earth on the Feast of Pentecost in the year 1300, and that the male dominated Papacy would then pass away, yielding to a line of female Popes. In preparation for this event they elected Sister Manfreda, to be the first of the Popesses, and several wealthy families of Lombardy provided at great cost the sacred vessels they expected her to use when she said Mass in Rome at the Church of Santa Maria Maggiore. Naturally, the Inquisition exterminated this new sect, and the "Popess" was burned at the stake in the autumn of 1300. Later the Inquisition proceeded against Matteo Visconti, the first Duke of Milan, for his connections with the sect.

Maifreda was an Abbess in the Umiliati Order and first cousin to Matteo Visconti, the Ghibelline (anti-pope) ruler of Milan. Maifreda believed the Holy Spirit had manifested on earth in the form of Guglielma (d. 1281), a middle-aged woman with a grown son who claimed to be a daughter of Premysl Otakar, King of Bohemia, and, who on arriving in Milan in 1260, donned a *"simple brown habit"* and lived the life of a saint. To the Guglielmites, her arrival fulfilled a prophecy of St. Joachim de Fiore that a new age of the Holy Spirit would begin in 1260,

> "Heralding the inauguration of an ecclesia spiritualis in which grace, spiritual knowledge and contemplative gifts would be diffused to all."

122

Although she vehemently denied it,

> "..*rumours of divinity already swirled around Guglielma during her lifetime.*"
>
> "*Her words about 'the body of the Holy Spirit,' together with her mysterious royal origins, Pentecostal birth, imputed healings and stigmata, coalesced to create a more-than-human mystique in the minds of her friends.*"

Immediately after her death dozens of portraits were painted and chapels were dedicated to Santa Guglielma.

Giotto Fides Barbara Newman (aka Mona Alice Jean Newman) presented the most complete account in English of the Guglielmites in her "*From Virile Woman to WomanChrist: Studies in Medieval Religion and Literature,*" but it is in her more recent paper, "*The Heretic Saint: Guglielma of Bohemia, Milan and Brunate,*" that we learn important details that make an attribution to Maifreda as Papess much stronger than previously thought (all quotes and information not otherwise attributed are from this article).

Andrea Vitali recounts a summary of the trial of Guglielma and her followers in which we find:

> "*As Christ was true God and true Man, in the same manner, she [Guglielma] claimed herself to be true God and true Man in the female sex, come to save the Jews, the Saracens and the false Christians, in the same way as the true Christians are saved by means of Christ.*"

(Tying her story in with the final cards of Judgment and the World, we find,)

> "*She too claimed she would arise again with a human body in the female sex before the final resurrection, in order to rise to heaven before the eyes of her disciples, friends and devotees.*"

Matteo Visconti (first Duke of Milan and first cousin to Maifreda) had as an advisor his good friend, Cary-Papess Francesco da Garbagnate, an ardent devotee of Guglielma. Matteo was at the centre of his own long battle with the Church, having expelled the Papal Inquisitors in 1311, and being himself excommunicated in 1317, tried for sorcery and heresy in 1321, and having Milan placed under interdict in 1322. Matteo's grandmother and uncle (archbishop of Milan) had earlier been named heretics.

From Newman's article, we learn that Maifreda's convent was founded in 1290 in Biassono, only five miles from the small town of Concorezzo the former home of the Concorezzo Cathars, who were burned as heretics or driven out by in 1230, only 60 years before. After the Albigensian crusade many small towns around Milan became refugee outposts of this faith, of which Concorezzo was a centre, and may have inspired the order of nuns who called themselves the *"humble"* (umiliati). Is this the beginning of The Church's fear driven misogyny?

The most compelling bit of data making this attribution of the Papess card almost certain is that between 1440 and 1460 Bianca Maria Visconti, wife of Francesco Sforza and duchess of Milan, frequently visited Maddalena Albrizzi, Abbess of monasteries in Como and Brunate, and gave aid and gifts to the Order. (Brunate is just north of Milan with Biassono between them). Even the stones for the Como monastery were donated by Francesco Sforza. The Visconti-Sforza deck was probably commissioned by or for Bianca Maria. Around 1450, at the same time the Visconti-Sforza deck was produced, a cycle of frescos were painted in the Church of San Andrea at Brunate that recorded the story of Guglielma:

> *"How she left the house of her husband, came to Brunate, and lived a solitary life here, wearing a hairshirt and ordinary dress . . . in the company of a crucifix and an image of Our Lady."*

Only one of these frescos, ornately framed, remains today near the original chapel that had been dedicated to Saint Guglielma. It depicts Guglielma with two figures kneeling before her. She appears to be giving a special blessing to a nun. Newman identifies the two as Maifreda and Andrea Saramita (he was the main promulgator of her divinity as the Holy Spirit). Others, more convincingly, claim them as Maddalena Albrizzi (founder of the monastery and candidate for sainthood) and her cousin Pietro Albrici who renovated the church. Even as late as the nineteenth century, Sir Richard Burton, author of The Arabian Nights, noted that:

> *"Santa Guglielma, worshipped at Brunate, works many miracles, chiefly healing aches of head."*

Furthermore, Guglielma's story and veneration were popularised in Ferrara by 1425 through a hagiography (saint's life) by Antonio Bonfadini, and in Florence through a popular late-15th century religious play by Antonia Pulci

It seems reasonable to conclude that Bianca Maria Visconti may have had a special devotion to the woman whom, 150 years after being condemned by the Inquisition, so many Lombards venerated as a saint, and that she honoured an earlier family member. Maifreda, who served as Guglielma's Vicar, hiding her in plain sight as an allegory of Faith. Bianca Maria Visconti would have seen this card as Maifreda, as would have her contemporaries.

Later European Protestant countries de-sacralised the deck, finding both The Pope and The Papess objectionable and substituting for them cards like Jupiter and Juno, Bacchus and the Spanish Captain, or the Moors. However, the archetype of the sacred feminine remains to this day in the taro deck as The Priestess card.

CPSIA information can be obtained
at www.ICGtesting.com
Printed in the USA
LVHW091601290121
677804LV00007B/281